A
HINDU FAMILY
IN BRITAIN

A HINDU FAMILY IN BRITAIN

Sauresh Ray

Headteacher, Hungerford Junior School, London

Religious and Moral Education Press
A Member of the BPCC Group

Religious and Moral Education Press
A Member of the BPCC Group
Hennock Road, Exeter EX2 8RP

Pergamon Press Ltd
Headington Hill Hall, Oxford OX3 0BW

Pergamon Press Inc.
Maxwell House, Fairview Park, Elmsford, New York 10523

Pergamon Press Canada Ltd
Suite 104, 150 Consumers Road, Willowdale, Ontario M2J 1P9

Pergamon Press (Australia) Pty Ltd
P.O. Box 544, Potts Point, N.S.W. 2011

Pergamon Press GmbH
Hammerweg 6, D–6242 Kronberg, Federal Republic of Germany

First published 1986

Printed in Great Britain by A. Wheaton & Co. Ltd, Hennock Road, Exeter

ISBN 0 08–031782–0 non net
ISBN 0 08–031783–9 net

Contents

To the beloved memory of Bhabesh Ray and to my mother

ACKNOWLEDGEMENTS

It would be impossible to mention individually all the people and organizations who helped in the production of this book, but the author wishes to thank the following for their generous contributions:

Nirmal Mukerji

Dilip Chatterjee

Jayashree Desai

Ana Rodriguez

Asha Shinh

S. B. Deshkar and the Hindu Centre, London

A. T. S. Ratnasingham and the Shree Ganapathy Temple, Wimbledon

Professor Bhikhu Parekh for his invaluable advice and guidance,
and for writing the Foreword

Alaka Ray for her support and involvement throughout

Author's Note

I would urge the reader to be aware that it is virtually impossible to show the multi-faceted nature of Hinduism through the eyes of a single family. Although the imaginary family in this book reflects Bengali culture, it nevertheless highlights many of the features common to family structures all over India.

I shall be happy if, while reading this book, generalization is avoided and the reader understands that Hinduism is a way of life whose complexity cannot be summed up in a single book, whatever its size and however painstaking the author.

Photographs are reproduced by kind permission of Alaka Ray, Sauresh Ray, Bury Peerless, Ray Bruce/CEM Video, Trustees of the British Museum, BBC Hulton Picture Library, Commonwealth Institute, Government of India Tourist Office, London, Victoria and Albert Museum, Torbay News Agency. Cover picture by Alaka Ray.

Line drawings by Ian Foulis and Associates and Sauresh Ray

vi

Foreword

It is not easy to write about "the Hindu family". Hindu society is divided into scores of major castes, sects and linguistic groups, and for several millenia has been subject to waves of foreign influences. Not surprisingly the structure of the Hindu family varies considerably, depending on whether and to what degree it is Westernized, whether it is an urban or rural, middle- or working-class family, and whether it belongs to a high or a low caste.

Another reason why it is difficult to describe the Hindu family has to do with the Hindus' distinctive manner of conceptualizing social relationships. In the West, since the nineteenth century (if not earlier) it has been taken for granted that men and women should develop along different lines, cultivate distinct emotional, moral and other qualities, and that men should at all costs avoid becoming "effeminate" and women "masculine". The Hindus have refused to draw the distinction or, at least, to draw it so rigidly. In their view the so-called manly and womanly qualities complement each other and form part of a coherent whole; without each other's regulative influence they become distorted.

Again, Western societies draw a fairly rigid distinction between childhood and adulthood and have added, during the last few decades, the intermediate stage of adolescence. Each of the three stages is deemed to be autonomous and to have its own distinctive demands and requirements. The Hindus cannot see why the process of growth from birth to death should be divided up into such neat and insulated stages, and tend to view the child as an adult in the making and the adult as someone who rightly retains some qualities of the child. Adulthood consists not in outgrowing but consolidating and building on childhood. These and other features of the Hindu family make it an extremely complex institution, and its nature and dynamics cannot easily be explained to the Western reader.

vii

Mr Sauresh Ray has discharged this difficult task with commendable skill. He fully appreciates that the Hindu family cannot be understood except in the context of Hindu philosophy and culture, and accordingly spends some time outlining these. He also recognizes that the Hindu family structures its perceptions of time and space, articulates its identity and continuity, and organizes its internal relationships in terms of a highly complex set of ceremonies, rituals and observances, and takes pains to explain these in some detail. As a result he manages to convey in clear and lucid terms much of the richness and complexity of the Hindu family. I am happy to recommend his book to all those interested in the subject.

Bhikhu Parekh

Professor of Political Theory, University of Hull,
and Deputy Chairman, Commission for Racial Equality

1
A Strange Custom

The corridor leading to the playground at Heathurst School soon filled up with noisy boys and girls when the bell rang for morning break. Everyone was rushing. As Anna stepped out of her classroom someone bumped into her and all her books went flying.

"Do you mind?" she shouted.

"Sorry," replied a distant voice melting into the crowd.

"Charming manners," muttered Anna as she started to pick up her books. One of them had landed right under the feet of a dark-haired boy hurrying along the corridor. He stopped to pick up the book, dusted it on his sleeve, touched it to his forehead and handed it to Anna. Then he rushed off. He did all this very quickly, as if by instinct.

"Thanks," said Anna, but the boy probably didn't hear her.

This incident seemed rather odd to Anna. All day she kept wondering why the boy had touched the book to his forehead. He had closed his eyes when he did it, too – but why? Her friends couldn't help her. One of them even tried to shut her up, saying, "Stop worrying about something so silly, Anna. It's nothing."

But to Anna it didn't seem silly at all. The gesture had meant something. That evening, she asked her father about it while he was watching the nine o'clock news. All she got in reply was, "In a minute, darling," so she knew she was wasting her time.

Her mother listened to the story and suggested, "Why don't you ask the boy himself?"

"Yes, I will, but I'll have to wait until I meet him again," Anna replied. "At the moment I know nothing about him – his name, or his class. He just appeared in front of me out of nowhere and dissolved into the crowd, leaving me with this puzzle."

Anna did not have to wait too long. Next morning, when she visited the school library, she saw the boy working in the reading

1

room. She couldn't believe her luck at finding the very person she wanted to see so easily, in a school of over twelve hundred pupils!

"Excuse me," she began. "May I disturb you for a minute, please?"

He looked up from his book and smiled. "Yes, certainly. I've seen you before somewhere, haven't I? I know – you dropped your books in the corridor yesterday, didn't you?"

"Well done," said Anna. "And you picked one up for me. Thanks again. Tell me, why did you touch the book to your forehead before giving it to me? By the way, my name's Anna. What's yours?"

"Goutam. Goutam Datta. Do you know, I can't remember doing that, but I suppose I must have. It's just a habit. You see, we Hindus are brought up to believe that books are sacred. Therefore, if we accidentally touch one with our feet, we apologize to our goddess by touching it to our forehead."

"That's very interesting. Can you tell me any more, please?"

"Well, every year we celebrate the worship of **Saraswati**, who is our goddess of learning and the arts. Books are amongst the objects placed at her feet to be blessed."

At this point the bell rang, interrupting their conversation. Before saying goodbye, Anna thanked Goutam for explaining the meaning of the gesture. She added that she would like to learn a bit more about his religion. The next day being Saturday, they agreed to meet at the library at Swiss Cottage.

2
Anna Prashan

During their meeting Goutam told Anna that he came to live in Britain seven years ago with his mother and his sister Sikha, who is also at Heathurst School. Anna said she hadn't realized that Goutam was related to Sikha, whom she knew by sight. Their father settled in Britain some years earlier and works as a chartered accountant. Their mother teaches at a local primary school. The Dattas are Hindus and live in Hampstead.

"I'll be honest with you, Anna," said Goutam. "I don't know enough about Hinduism to be able to discuss it as a subject, but I am familiar with a lot of our customs and practices. I remember my childhood in India and know that most of my beliefs come from what I learned by following my elders and our traditions. I also learned about our gods and goddesses through stories my grandparents told me, and the children's books I read.

"I suggest that you attend a Hindu celebration. You will find the experience very interesting. Besides, Hinduism is such a vast and complex subject that it is best to look at it from within. The more you become involved, the more you will understand.

"I can think of a family celebration which will take place in three weeks' time," Goutam went on. "It is called **Anna Prashan**. One of our friends' six-month-old boy is to be initiated into rice-eating. In other words, the child will be offered, for the very first time, the food normally eaten by adults. It will be a social and religious occasion, and, like all Hindu ceremonies, will be performed with many wonderful rituals."

"What sort of rituals?" asked Anna.

"Little things: what to touch, where to sit, which way to look – all the details observed with great care during such ceremonies. They may seem strange to an outsider, but are really fascinating once you begin to understand why they are being performed. Try to come," Goutam urged Anna, "you'll enjoy it."

3

"I'm sure I shall," answered Anna, "but I must ask my parents first."

"Yes, of course," agreed Goutam. "I too must ask my parents, although I'm quite sure they won't object."

The three weeks passed quickly. Both Goutam and Anna obtained permission from their parents, and Goutam introduced Anna to his sister. The two girls became good friends.

One Saturday afternoon Anna arrived at Belsize Park underground station as arranged. Goutam and Sikha were waiting for her.

Sikha greeted her, "Well done, Anna! Very punctual. The church isn't far from here, just ten minutes' walk away."

"Church?" Anna was rather surprised. "I thought you didn't go to church."

Goutam laughed and explained that it wasn't the church itself they were going to but the reception annexe, where community activities take place. "On occasions like this, well over a hundred guests are invited. In India the celebrations would happen at home, but here people usually hire a hall, because their houses are too small."

On the way Goutam stopped outside the former Hampstead Town Hall and said to Anna, "Mark this place, too: another popular venue. Every October hundreds of people come here to celebrate the festival of **Durga Puja**."

They were soon at the church hall, where Anna was warmly received by Mr and Mrs Datta.

Mr Datta told her, "I have heard a lot about you, Anna. Goutam and Sikha tell me you are interested in our customs. Well, I am most impressed to hear that. You are very welcome."

Mrs Datta embraced her and said, "Welcome, my dear. I am delighted to meet you. Come with me. I shall introduce you to a few people. You must greet them by joining your hands together and saying '**Namaskaar**' (Greetings), like this."

As Mrs Datta demonstrated, Anna smiled and nodded. She started to feel at home and soon found herself in the company of a group of young girls who were friends of Sikha's. There were children running around excitedly. Language was no problem. Anna noticed that the children and young people spoke mostly in English although their parents were speaking an Indian language which, she gathered, was Bengali.

4

A lot of people were already there and more were arriving. The women wore beautiful saris and jewellery and looked elegant in their distinctive hair-styles. Only one of the men wore Indian dress: a spotless white lower garment called a **dhoti** and a **kurta**, or tunic; the rest were in Western clothes.

The hall was beautifully decorated with paper-chains and many attractive cut-out Oriental wall decorations. A large square section of the floor had been painted with liquid white chalk; this was an **alpana** pattern. It looked like a giant carpet. In the middle of the square was a small, dark-coloured mat with vases of flowers on either side. This was where the main ceremony would take place. A recording of sitar music played softly and trails of smoke billowed from smouldering incense sticks. People bustled about attending to various details. Anna was totally absorbed in the unique atmosphere.

Traditional South Indian alpana pattern

Suddenly someone cried, "They've arrived!" Anna looked out of a window and saw that a car had pulled up outside. A young couple stepped out. The mother was carrying a lovely baby in her arms. Mrs Datta came over and asked Anna to join the others; they were going to welcome the new arrivals.

"This is Anna, my daughter's friend," said Mrs Datta. Then she turned to Anna and introduced Mr and Mrs Ghosh. "This is little Partha," she added, "in whose honour the reception is being held."

Anna felt very shy, but managed to smile and say "Namaskaar" properly. Partha was dressed in a miniature version of a proper dhoti and kurta and his forehead was decorated with a pattern made from sandalwood paste. There was a large black dot between his eyebrows and his eyelids were lined with **kajal** (a black powder). He looked like a six-month-old bridegroom!

As the auspicious moment approached Partha was carried to the mat by his mother and helped to sit up. In front of him, on a large silver plate, there was a mound of cooked rice surrounded by dishes of fish, meat and vegetables. All round the plate were twenty or so silver bowls containing delicious curries and sweets. Anna counted thirty-six different items altogether!

"That's right," confirmed Mrs Datta. "Thirty-six. That is the custom. But don't worry. Partha won't eat even one of them. The food is just an offering to the child. He will simply sit there and look at it."

Mrs Ghosh handed the child to the man dressed in Indian style. He was a friend who, in the absence of a maternal uncle, would perform the act of feeding (this is usually the duty of the mother's brother). It is considered inauspicious for the mother to watch, so Mrs Ghosh had to leave the scene.

Although there was no formal act of worship, the blessings of Lord **Lakshmi-Narayan** were invoked. Then a spoonful of specially prepared rice pudding – a **prasaad**, or offering, to Lord Lakshmi-Narayan – was put in the child's mouth with a beautiful silver spoon from a dainty silver bowl. The spoon and the bowl were gifts sent to Partha by his grandparents in India.

As the first taste of the delicious pudding was absorbed in his mouth, little Partha looked puzzled and surprised. Then his eyes began to shine with delight and he struggled to reach for the second spoonful. This was the moment everyone was waiting for.

6

The music playing in the background was drowned by thunderous applause. The child had accepted the food! Mrs Ghosh rushed forward again and picked up her son, who had gracefully performed his first adult role!

The second part of the ceremony was even more interesting: a tray holding a number of different articles, each symbolizing a different occupation, was placed in front of the child. There was a book (representing a writer or scholar), a flower (artist or botanist), a bell (artist or musician), gold (wealthy person), a brush, a pen and so on. The idea was that the child would naturally be attracted to one of the items on the tray and pick it up. According to custom, his choice would determine his future career. People take this ritual quite seriously, and the whole family comes to watch.

Partha picked up the pen and, while everyone was busy congratulating his parents that he would become a great scholar, he put it straight into his mouth, as if to show that he had just been given the go-ahead to eat whatever he liked!

The baby has chosen a pen. Will he be a scholar one day?

At the end of the ceremony they all sat down to a magnificent meal. When it was time to leave they each gave the child a present.

Anna was thrilled by the celebration. Mr and Mrs Datta and the others laughed when she told them that for her, like Partha, it had been an introduction to Indian food, and that she too thought it absolutely delicious! Mr Datta invited her to visit them some time so that he could tell her more about Hindu customs.

3
Religion in Daily Life

It was a Sunday afternoon and Sikha's fifteenth birthday. She had invited Anna to her house. The two friends were talking in her room while Goutam watched television downstairs. Mr and Mrs Datta were both busy preparing the food and there was a tantalizing aroma in the air. Apart from the sounds of cooking and conversation in the kitchen and the noise from the television, Anna thought that the house seemed unusually quiet for a birthday celebration.

"When are the others coming?" she asked.

"What others? There won't be anyone else. You are the guest of honour today," replied Sikha.

"Oh no!" Anna exclaimed, embarrassed.

Sikha reassured her: "You see, we used to celebrate every birthday with a party. Since we arrived in Britain I've had three of them, but I don't seem to have the urge any more. My brother hasn't had a single birthday party since we've been here! We now remember each other's birthdays by doing what we used to do in India.

"Over there I would have a bath in the morning and my mother would give me a set of new clothes to wear. Then I would offer my prayers to our family deity, by offering a fresh flower and a sweet and lighting an incense stick. I would kneel in front of the image of the deity, join my palms and pray. My mother would dip her ring-finger in a plate of yoghurt and put a dot on my forehead, saying, 'May you live long'. To acknowledge her blessing I would touch her feet, and then accept a sweet from the deity's prasaad before running off to play and show off my new dress. Come, I'll show you our family deities."

Sikha took Anna into her parents' bedroom. It was a large, beautifully furnished room. In one corner, by the window, there

Worship at a family shrine in Britain

was a shelf on which stood several statues and framed paintings of gods and goddesses. Sikha introduced them to her. There was **Lakshmi**, the goddess of fortune; **Shiva**, the lord of destruction; **Ganesha**, the god of wisdom and the remover of obstacles; Lord **Krishna** (a form of **Lord Vishnu**), worshipped for continuity and permanence; **Radha**, Krishna's consort; **Kali** and **Durga**, who are different forms of the Divine Mother who rose to free the world from the forces of evil, and **Saraswati**, the goddess of learning and the arts.

Anna was surprised. "You have a lot of gods and goddesses in your religion, haven't you? Some of them look very strange! That one has an elephant's head, and this goddess has ten arms!"

"There are said to be three hundred and thirty million Hindu deities," replied Sikha. "It is impossible for anyone to know them all, so we choose a few favourites to worship as family deities."

"How do you choose?"

"I knew you would ask that!" laughed Sikha. "Well, there are lots of stories about our gods and goddesses. The stories are fascinating, and the characters are so true to life that we are drawn to them from an early age. Our gods and goddesses are like real

A charming picture of the goddess Lakshmi from West Bengal

Painting of the sacred mouse, vehicle of Ganesha

people to us, very powerful people who came down from their heavenly homes and involved themselves in the affairs of human beings whenever they thought it was necessary. Sometimes they took part in battles, or disguised themselves as ordinary people – in order to enter a household and test someone's honesty, kindness or bravery, for example, or to find out whether they had any weaknesses, such as cruelty or vanity. The stories tell us how our deities took on different roles to help good overcome evil, or to banish poverty, illness and other forms of suffering from the daily lives of their devotees (their faithful followers)."

"Why do you keep your deities in here?" asked Anna.

"Yes, why indeed?" sighed Sikha. She explained: "In our family home in India, where my grandmother and other relations still live, we have a whole room to use as a family shrine. All our deities are kept there. Every morning the floor is washed, fresh alpana is drawn on it, flowers are picked and all the items used for the daily worship, or **puja**, are brought out and cleaned. Over here we don't have a whole room to spare for the deities, but my mother would never settle down anywhere without them. This seemed the most sensible place to install them. The idea is to select a convenient place in the house, somewhere that is kept perfectly clean and is unlikely to be disturbed too often."

At this point Goutam appeared and announced that the meal was ready.

The table looked very impressive. There were a lot of different dishes and each one looked delicious. While they sat down, Goutam explained to Anna that they do not say prayers before every meal. He described a ritual his grandfather in India used to perform before eating in order to thank Lord Vishnu for the food:

"He would cup his right hand and tip a little water from his own glass into it. He sipped the water three times, saying, 'Nama Vishnu', which means 'I bow to thee, Lord Vishnu', and sprinkled the water around his plate. He would also take a pinch of every item of food and put it aside. At the end of the meal, he would give this to the birds or to the fish in the pond, to share his food with other creatures."

Mr Datta was amused by Goutam's demonstration of his grandfather's routine. "Well, Goutam," he said, "since we have Anna as our guest, and it is your sister's birthday, why don't we begin by wishing Sikha a happy birthday?"

They all agreed and sang "Happy Birthday" to Sikha before they began to eat.

Still thinking of the ritual Goutam had described, Anna asked him, "How could your grandfather throw food to the fish, Goutam? We throw breadcrumbs to the birds in our garden, but fish? Is there a fish-pond in your garden?"

"Oh no," laughed Goutam, "not like the one you have in mind, but a very big one, like a swimming-pool, with lots of fish. I learned to swim in it, and after our festivals the images of the gods and goddesses are immersed in it, too."

Mr Datta said, "Our family home is in a village and the way of life there is so different that whatever we do or say needs to be carefully explained, Anna, so that you may understand, although we take it all for granted. You could learn a lot by simply walking through a village in Bengal, where we come from. Since we can't take you there in person, perhaps we should introduce our village by telling you a little bit about it. Would you like that?"

"Yes, please, I would," replied Anna.

"Very well," said Mr Datta. "I'll start, and the others can contribute from time to time." He paused to collect his thoughts. "There is a temple of Shiva not far from our house where the first puja of the day is offered by the resident priest at exactly five o'clock every morning. The whole village wakes up as the bells ring out and the priest's voice is clearly heard from the shrine of the temple. 'Om Nama Shivaya' (We bow to thee, Lord Shiva) he chants.

"The puja coincides with the rising of the sun. The temple stands on the bank of a river and is surrounded by enormous banyan trees. Their trailing roots hang down like the matted locks of a **sadhu**, or holy man. The temple is a beautiful sight, and has always created in our hearts a feeling of awe and wonder. As you go nearer, the sound of the chanting of **mantras** (hymns) and the tolling of the bell greet you. The atmosphere is one of peace and holiness.

"Throughout the day, beginning from that early hour, men, women and children go down to the river. While they bathe, many duck under the water several times, calling out the name of the Lord. Others take handfuls of water and make gestures of offering to the sun, the source of energy and all life-forms. The **Brahmins** perform more rituals than the other bathers."

14

Temple of Shiva under a banyan tree

Children washing their feet before entering a temple

"Who are they?" asked Anna. "And why do they perform more rituals than the rest?"

"The Brahmins are a special group among the Hindus," replied Mrs Datta. "We'll talk about the groups another time, though. For the time being let us concentrate on village life. As we go along you will see that almost everything we do has a religious basis, however slight."

Mr Datta continued, "The bathers then change into dry clothes. Many of the women go home balancing a brass or earthenware pitcher filled with water on their hip. Some of the men carry a smaller pitcher or bucket of water to pour over the temple deity while chanting hymns of praise. Others return to their family shrine, picking a bunch of flowers on the way which they will offer to their own deities.

"Our house is made of brick with a flat roof. Only three other houses in the village are made in the same way. The others have mud walls and thatched roofs. In most houses the rooms are arranged around a courtyard and there is a raised verandah at the front. During festivals the walls are decorated with delicate patterns drawn with rice-paste or paint.

"Early in the morning the housewives and young girls sprinkle water over the courtyards and pathways and sweep them briskly with a hard broom. They draw holy patterns on the doorstep with their fingers, using rice-paste. These patterns represent the footsteps of the goddess Lakshmi. They are also drawn around the large brick plant-pot where the tulsi plant grows."

"I'm sorry to interrupt you again, but what is a tulsi plant?" enquired Anna.

Mr Datta explained that tree- and plant-worship has been popular with Hindus for centuries. The banyan and the pipul trees are sacred.

"These are huge trees, but the tulsi is only a small, bushy plant which grows to no more than a metre in height," he told Anna. "Its leaves are oval and the branches are a mixture of brown, green and purple. It is considered the most sacred of all plants and is also believed to be a form of Lakshmi, wife of Lord Vishnu. That's why the tulsi plant is grown with such care in practically every Hindu household.

"Meanwhile, as the morning progresses, more activities take place. Those children who attend school go off to have bath, either

16

in the river or in a pond, or, if they have a deep well or a tube-well, they sit by the well and pour water over themselves from a bucket. After that they put a square mat, called an **asan**, or a board called a **pidi**, made of wooden planks, on the floor and sit down to a simple meal. This usually consists of boiled rice, some **dal** (lentils or other pulses), some vegetables and a little fish."

Roadside temple with a tulsi plant in the forecourt

Goutam said, "We used to walk to school carrying our books and slates in a hessian bag. Although the school was only a couple of kilometres from our house, Sikha used to complain every day that her legs were tired or she had a headache."

Anna grinned as Sikha protested, "Well, you are older than me. Besides, you were always in such a hurry that you made me run."

"That's true, but it was only to get you away from the shrine as quickly as possible, remember?" replied Goutam.

"Which shrine?" asked Mrs Datta curiously.

"As we walked along the river-bank," Goutam told her, "we used to pass the wayside shrine under the large pipul tree. Every morning the villagers came there to worship the pillar-shaped stone representing Lord Shiva and the lovely statue of **Nandi**, the bull Lord Shiva rides. They used to smear the deities with sandalwood paste and vermilion – a bright red dye – and leave tiny pots of milk, flowers and sweets as their offerings.

Nandi

18

"After the worshippers had left, two or three squirrels would come down from the branches of the tree and make good use of the offerings. Sikha spent hours looking at them. She became very cross if I spoke to her. The squirrels got used to seeing her there and let her come quite close to the shrine.

"One morning I was waiting while Sikha watched the squirrels. Suddenly she let out a piercing scream. I rushed over and held her tight. She had covered her face with her hands but was still looking through her fingers. She was shaking like a leaf! When I glanced at the shrine I too became paralysed with fear. Instead of the timid squirrels, I saw a huge cobra, coiled around the stone figures. It was looking me straight in the eye.

"Sikha's scream had attracted other children on their way to school, and some boys picked up sticks and stones and approached the shrine. Sikha and I moved away because we didn't want to see the snake being killed.

"Just then the fisherman from our village appeared on the scene. He drove the boys away, saying, 'The cobra and the bull are Shiva's favourite creatures. If you kill that snake at the Lord's own shrine you will be committing a sin for which you will not be forgiven. Besides, today is **Naga Panchami** day, when serpents are worshipped, not killed. You call yourselves pupils, but you don't seem to have learned very much.'

"We, too, felt a bit ashamed as we had no idea it was Naga Panchami day. The fisherman sat down, ready to protect the cobra if the boys returned, and began muttering mantras. After a while the huge snake uncoiled itself and slowly slithered away down the slope of the river-bank. We never went to that shrine again."

Mr Datta seemed a bit concerned. "You never told me that story before," he said quietly.

"Thank God you didn't come to any harm," added Mrs Datta, automatically joining her hands and bowing her head.

It was nearly six o'clock. Anna's parents arrived to collect her. As they wanted to wish Sikha a happy birthday, Mrs Datta invited them in and offered them a cup of coffee.

Mr Datta continued, "You see, even in that chilling story there is a religious element. Our children didn't know it was Naga Panchami day because it is an occasion our family doesn't celebrate, although we respect the tradition. The fisherman knew because he was also a farmer. No farmer would plough his land on

19

this day for fear of hurting a snake while furrowing the ground and incurring the wrath of **Manasha,** the goddess of the serpents.

"To return to what we were saying earlier," he went on, "as the children leave for school, the adults set off for work. Most of them travel either on foot, by bus from the main road, in a rickshaw or by bicycle. It is not uncommon to see a holy symbol like the ancient sign of the **swastika** drawn even on these means of transport. Their owners believe that mechanical objects also need the blessings of **Lord Viswarkarma** and Ganesha to function properly.

"Children start their education at the age of three or four. They are initiated during the **Saraswati Puja** celebrations through a ceremony called **Hate Khadi.** They learn to read from a book called the *Varna Parichaya*, which literally means 'knowing the alphabets'. There are other books, but this one is very popular. The children always read aloud. As soon as they can read a little they become familiar with passages in the *Varna Parichaya* like this one (from page 16 of the book):

'It is dawn. Crows are cawing. Rise, and wash your mouth. Sit down to learn.'

"Or, later (on page 26):

'Birds sing as the night comes to its end.
In the garden, the flowers come into bloom.
The sun rises, and the sky reddens with its hue.
Every heart is joyous as the light is received on earth.'

"From a tender age children are influenced by such descriptions of nature. They are able to appreciate the elements through their own experience. They feel the presence of Mother Nature or the Goddess of Nature in the world around them. A sense of respect grows in them.

"The children return from school in the afternoon and have a snack. This may be pitha (home-made cake), moodi (like crispies), khai (puffed rice) or chide (pressed rice). They are eaten with sugar-cane syrup, molasses, sugar or fruit, such as mangoes.

"Pitha is made in different ways according to the festive occasions of the year. The most important of these is probably **Makar Sankranti. Makar** is the sign of Capricorn and **Sankranti** is

20

the period when the sun leaves one sign of the zodiac and enters another. This is a holy occasion, when the sun is worshipped. In every household a whole range of pitha is made of rice and sweet potatoes with all sorts of mouth-watering stuffings, sweet and savoury.

"When they have eaten, the children go out to play. Play-acting is a popular game. This takes place in the courtyard of the temple or in the village square, which is another large open space in front of the temple of our village deity, our **grama devata**. All the major festivals are celebrated here, either in the open or under a special canopy called the **shamiana**. Children act out themes or scenes from religious stories or legends of the kings and queens of Hindu mythology.

Village deity under a pipul tree being worshipped at Makar Sankranti

21

"Their play ends – in fact, all the activities of the day end – the moment the priest is seen to enter the threshold of the shrine. He lights a brass oil-lamp called a **pradip**, rings his **ghanta**, or cowbell, and calls out: 'Om Nama Shivaya'. Then he proceeds with the rituals of the Lord's evening worship.

"The other bells ring out. The sun goes down. The sky and the patches of cloud floating in it are splashed with many shades of red, yellow and grey. The silhouetted shapes of the trees, the houses and the temple look like a gigantic canvas painted by a great artist. As darkness gradually engulfs the village, the sound of conch shells is heard from every household. A pradip is lit at every tulsi tree and family shrine. Dusk, like dawn, is a very auspicious moment.

"Although it is only early evening, the whole world seems to be blanketed in silence. But when you walk through the village, following the paths that weave in and out of the clusters of houses, you can hear voices: people gossiping on their verandahs, groups of men playing cards, and the sound of sacred verses being read aloud from the two great epic poems: the **Ramayana** and the **Mahabharata**. There are also the **Lakshmi Purana**, which include the stories of the goddess Lakshmi and other folk-songs and stories.

"In my opinion, these stories provide the basis for the Hindu child's understanding of his or her religion. Even at my age I find myself drawn to them, such is their intoxicating charm! In order to understand India and Hinduism one should be familiar with our villages and their culture. Mahatma Gandhi said, 'Go to the villages: that is India, therein lives the soul of India.'"

"That was wonderful," said Anna softly after a short silence. "I simply cannot tell you how much I have enjoyed being here with you today. And that lovely meal!"

Her father remarked, "I can now see why my daughter is always talking about you and India. You have brought tears to my eyes, Mr Datta, because you have made me remember my childhood in the country village where I grew up. You must all come and visit us some time."

The Dattas thanked him, and asked Anna to come again soon for their next session on India and Hinduism.

22

SIGNS OF THE ZODIAC

The Western and the Hindu zodiac are the same, with one exception. The sign of Capricorn, the goat, is interpreted as Makar, the King of Fish. Makar is the vehicle of Goddess Ganga (Mother Ganges) and appears as a huge and powerful water creature with the head of an elephant and the body of a fish. Because of its ferocious nature, some people think it is like a shark, while others see it as a crocodile.

Mesha		Aries	**Tula**		Libra
Brisha		Taurus	**Brischik**		Scorpio
Mithuna		Gemini	**Dhanu**		Sagittarius
Karkata		Cancer	**Makar**		Capricorn
Singha		Leo	**Kumbha**		Aquarius
Kanya		Virgo	**Meena**		Pisces

QUESTIONS AND PROJECTS

Chapters 1–3

1 Hindus regard all books as sacred. How do people of other faiths show respect for their holy books?

2 Why is the Anna Prashan ceremony important?

3 What musical instruments might be played at a Hindu ceremony? Find out which instruments are most often used in the religious celebrations of other major religions.

4 Draw a picture of a shrine in a traditional Hindu household, in India or in Britain. What religious artefacts (objects or pictures) might you find in a Muslim, Christian or Jewish home?

5 Describe a birthday celebration in your family.

6 A ritual some Hindus perform before eating is described in Chapter 3. Can you think of any similar practices in other religions?

7 Working in small groups, draw up lists of foods that are associated with special times of the year. Choose at least two different faiths.

8 In Greek and Roman legends gods and goddesses sometimes disguise themselves in order to become involved in the lives of human beings. Read some of these legends. Do they have anything in common with present-day stories about imaginary heroes and heroines like Superman and Wonder Woman?

9 Write a short play about a superhuman being who comes to live on earth as an ordinary person.

10 Speaking of daily life in a Hindu village, Mrs Datta said, "Almost everything we do has a religious basis". Do you think this is true? Select examples from Chapter 3 to support your answer.

4
The Origins of Hinduism

One day a new girl arrived in Anna's class. She was an Indian girl from Uganda called Sumitra. When Mr Smith, the history teacher, introduced her to the class, Anna welcomed her with the greeting the Dattas had taught her.

"Namaskaar," she said, and added, "Tumi kamon achho, Sumitra?" (How are you, Sumitra?)

In the past, this greeting had been much appreciated by Anna's other Indian friends, but Sumitra didn't respond at all. She didn't even look at Anna again, but simply walked to her seat and sat down, looking rather unhappy. Anna felt a little offended too, and the rest of the class thought Sumitra seemed an unfriendly sort of girl.

During the dinner break Anna and some of her friends were sitting on a bench in the playground when Sikha came over to join them. They told her about the new girl, and noticing that Anna was a bit upset, Sikha decided to change the subject and try to cheer her up. "Shall I tell you a story my father told me?" she suggested.

"Oh yes," they all answered.

Since they seemed enthusiastic, Sikha began, "Nearly three hundred years ago there lived a barber called Gopal who was endowed with a razor-sharp wit and shrewdness to match. He not only solved many impossible problems for his master, Raja Krishna Chandra, at whose court he was the jester, but helped many others who came to him.

"One day, in the capital city of Krishnanagar where Gopal lived, a mystery man appeared. He was absolutely fluent in several languages and a master of disguise. Almost every day he would speak in a different language, change his costume and make-up and go about the town pretending to be a different person from another part of the country. At first people were merely curious, but later they became suspicious of this stranger in their midst. They did their best to reveal the man's true identity, but in vain. He was polite to everyone. He always apologized, either in words or by gesture, if he didn't understand someone. He did nothing wrong, but his odd habit of changing his appearance made everyone uneasy. The townspeople went to Gopal and asked for his advice.

"Gopal listened carefully to what they had to say. Then he thought for a moment and asked them to come back in a week's time. When they returned, he told them triumphantly, 'Your mystery man comes from Orissa!'

"They were all very impressed. 'Really! How did you find out?' they asked.

"'Simple,' said Gopal, 'I just followed him everywhere and found out where he lived. Yesterday evening, when he was returning home in one of his ridiculous costumes, I came out of the dark alley by the corner shop and walked straight into him, pretending I hadn't seen him. He was so startled that he swore at me – in Oriya – "You blind bat! Why don't you watch where you're going?" And I said to him "Aha! Now I know, Brother, that you are a native of the land of our Lord Jagannath!" You see, when people are taken by surprise they always cry out in their mother tongue.' Next morning the stranger was gone!"

The girls laughed and said, "That was a good story, Sikha!"

"Thanks," she replied. "I remembered it when you were talking about Sumitra. Somehow I feel that you have misunderstood her. She too was upset at being put in a difficult and embarrassing situation. I'm sure she did not understand what you said, Anna, and could not respond. Besides, she must have been puzzled to be greeted like that by Anna, someone she expected to hear speaking only English. There are so many languages in India, you see, that people from different regions often do not understand one another."

Anna looked thoughtful. "I must admit, I hadn't considered that," she said.

Anna spent the following weekend with the Dattas. Mrs Datta had invited her to stay so that she could tell her a bit more about India. When Anna told them about Sumitra and the story of Gopal

26

Mr Datta smiled and said that Gopal, the witty barber of Krishnanagar, is a folk-hero. His stories are very popular with people of every age.

"India is such a vast country, with so many different types of people of different faiths and different languages, living in all sorts of climates and geographical conditions, that you simply cannot generalize and say that anything is typically 'Indian'," he continued. "Yet, as people of one country, one nation, they are all bound together as 'Indians'."

Mr Datta brought out a map of India to show Anna. "Just look at this map – it's like a piece of patchwork! Each of these 'patches' is a state. There are twenty-two states and well over six hundred million people. More than eighty per cent of the population are Hindus. So, although the inhabitants of Kashmir, Gujarat, Kerala, Assam and Manipur may be very different in their appearance and culture, a great number of them are Hindus."

"How did so many different people come to live in India in the first place, and how did they acquire so many languages?" asked Anna.

"Good question!" replied Mr Datta. "It's a very long story. The people of India can be broadly divided into four groups on the basis of their physical appearance and language. The **Aryans** are tall and fair-complexioned with an aquiline nose. Their languages are derived from **Sanskrit**. The word Sanskrit means 'perfected', which implies that it was a form of language perfected by the Aryans. Most Hindus from the upper social order belong to the Aryan group. The **Dravidians** are mostly the inhabitants of the southern parts of India. They are darker than the Aryans. The third group comprises the tribes who live in the hills and the forests. These primitive dwellers are very dark, short-statured and muscular and their languages are very different from those of the other two. In the last category are those with Mongoloid features: a slightly yellowish complexion, broad nose and narrow eyes. They live in the foothills of the Himalayas and the north-eastern parts of the country.

"We have also had visitors from outside: Greeks, Moguls, Huns, Arabs, Persians and, much later, the British, French and Dutch. All these people have mingled in India for thousands of years. The inter-mixing of races has resulted in the birth and development of many languages. The original tribes of India had

27

their own language before the Aryans arrived, and traces of it remain in the tribal languages of today: Kol, Santhal, Vil and so on. The languages spoken in the southern parts of India – Telegu, Tamil, Malayalam and Kannada – were influenced by the early Dravidians, whereas the North-Indian languages, like Hindi, Gujarati and Bengali, and Marathi (from South West India) were influenced by the Aryans. Following the arrival of the Muslims, Persian was exposed to the already existing Hindi and the Urdu language also began to develop. There are, in all, fourteen principal language groups who, between them, speak well over a thousand dialects."

Mr Datta paused for a moment as Anna said sadly, "Poor Sumitra! I had no idea that I was being so unfair to her. I greeted her in Bengali, a language she probably didn't even know."

Goutam said, "When I was at school in India, a young teacher used to take us for social studies and history. Like the stranger in that Gopal story, he too was fluent in four languages. He used to say that a mere lifetime is not enough to know India properly. Like the languages, many social customs and religious practices have evolved through the inter-mixing of the different groups of people. There are Hindus, Muslims, Buddhists, Jains, Sikhs, Christians, Parsees and others, all living side by side in this enormous land. That is why the Indians are, on the whole, so very tolerant of each other's faiths."

Mr Datta agreed. "Your teacher was quite right," he said. "Although from time to time there have been misunderstandings between the communities and violent exchanges have taken place, reconciliation has come about quickly and the people have continued to live in peace and harmony. It is, therefore, important that any outsider interested in our culture should understand that there are significant differences in all our customs and practices in various parts of the country.

"From the earliest times Indians have shared a deep sense of unity. The successive dynasties that ruled in India through the Ancient period and the Middle Ages all tried to unify the country during their reigns. In a political sense this unification was achieved by the Moguls and also by the British, who ruled India through a central government and introduced the same laws and currency for the whole country. But, as far as religion and culture are concerned, the entire subcontinent has remained as diverse as

28

Akbar praying on the bank of the River Indus, 1572. During the reign of this great Mogul emperor India became a united country.

ever. At the core of the Indian character is a desire to maintain unity in diversity."

At this point Mrs Datta appeared with a tray of snacks and tea.

"What a lovely way to interrupt!" remarked Sikha, and Mr Datta added, "I was getting thirsty, too."

The caste system

Mrs Datta asked Anna, "Has anyone answered the questions you asked about the Brahmins the other day?"

Mr Datta picked up his cup of tea and said, "Not yet, but I was just going to. First of all, Anna, you must understand India's caste system. The Aryans arrived in India as peace-loving settlers. They were a society of equals. As time went on, however, they moved further into the country in order to expand their territories. They had to fight the inhabitants who resisted their progress. Many battles were fought, but in between the wars the Aryans mingled with the non-Aryans, although they considered them to be inferior and referred to them as 'blacks', 'slaves' or 'robbers'. For the first time their society was divided according to the colour of people's skin.

"In the course of time, the Aryans began to feel the need to classify people according to their work. Those who were engaged in the study of religious scriptures and performed the pujas and sacrifices were known as **Brahmins**. Those involved in military affairs were called **Kshatriyas**. The **Vaishyas** were engaged in trade and the cultivation of land. A fourth group was formed of those who were the servants of the other three. They were called **Shudras**. These broad groups, known as 'castes', became completely self-sufficient units and the caste system as we know it was introduced.

"At first, society flourished under this system, but as time passed the Brahmins and the Kshatriyas – particularly the Brahmins, because of their association with the scriptures and religious matters – began to assume a position of importance. They called themselves **Varna Shrestha**, the 'highest caste'.

"The system became extremely rigid and strict rules were made. A person born into one caste could not change to another. Gradually the higher castes began to take advantage of the lower castes and even branded some as **Untouchables**."

30

Anna was shocked. "Do you mean that those people are actually separated from everyone else?" she exclaimed.

"Sikha answered, "Yes, they are. In our village, my grandmother still thinks of them as Untouchables."

"Why? Who are they?" asked Anna.

"Well," replied Goutam, "I know a family of so-called Untouchables in our village. They are very poor and usually work as scavengers, clearing drains and sewers. They also deal with hides, which they take from the carcasses of dead animals. No other castes do those kinds of work. Mind you, they too are Hindus and worship the same deities as we do. The only occasions that I can remember when, despite their lowly status, they took part in a community celebration were times when they were commissioned to play the drums at religious festivals and wedding ceremonies. They are skilful drummers.

"I can understand how you feel about the Untouchables, Anna, but you would be surprised to see how they accept their humble position with pride and dignity. Mahatma Gandhi revolted against the inhuman practice of Untouchability and called the Untouchables '**Harijans**', or 'children of God'. A Bengali poet wrote a remarkable poem elevating their position:

Whoever calls you untouchable, unclean, my friend?
Sanctity follows wherever you go,
Cleanliness persists with you in the midst of
                    our dwelling
Or else, man would long have returned to the wilds.

"Another poet, perhaps the greatest of them all, **Rabindra Nath Tagore**, wrote this powerful message for the nation:

O my unfortunate country,
    Those you have humiliated, those you have denied
        Their rights as humans;
Those that have stood in front of you,
    Instead of you seating them on your lap;
        Through humiliation alone you will be brought
To their lowly level."

"How wonderful!" said Anna. "Both poems are most inspiring – and reassuring."

Mr Datta continued: "With the growth of education this system has started to loosen its grip on modern Hindu society, but its influence is still very obvious, particularly in the villages. However, inter-caste marriages do happen and today many from the lower castes have privileged positions in government and in business, for example.

"In India, there are now laws which prevent people from practising Untouchability. But, unfortunately, the idea remains, especially in the minds of the older generation, some of whom find it difficult to break away from this habit. It has lasted more than a thousand years, after all.

"The Brahmins continue to dominate the field of worship. They conduct pujas in temples and shrines and at family ceremonies like weddings and **shraadhs**. The shraadh is a ceremony performed in honour of the dead. Many Brahmins, however, have gone into other vocations, ranging from agriculture to medicine and trade. Some are even employed as cooks by well-to-do families. Among the Hindus living in Britain today, you will find people belonging to all four castes and their numerous sub-castes."

Anna said, "I can see why you could not answer my question the other day. Caste is a vast subject. Another question has occurred to me. I would like to know who founded Hinduism."

Brahmin priests at a temple in Cuttack, Orissa, resting at midday

32

Mr Datta smiled and said, "The answer to that is 'Nobody', but a simple answer like that needs to be explained. Since you are spending the weekend with us, shall we leave it till tomorrow morning?"

The beginnings of Hinduism

The next morning, Anna woke up to the sound of a bell. It was Mrs Datta performing her morning worship. She realized that Sikha and Goutam would already be preparing breakfast and Mr Datta was probably waiting for her. Hurriedly she got ready, and as she came downstairs she was greeted with a chorus of "Good morning, Anna!"

Sikha added, "We did not want to disturb you so early on a Sunday morning. It is only half past seven! Daddy said that we ought to make an early start, and later on he would like to show you some of his slides from India."

"That sounds exciting!" Anna replied.

As they settled down in the lounge after breakfast, Mr Datta began: "Last night you must have been intrigued, Anna, to learn that Hinduism has no founder."

"You are absolutely right, Mr Datta," she replied. "It's hard to imagine that an old and important faith like Hinduism started without a founder."

"Yes, it's a unique religion in that respect," said Mr Datta. "The word 'Hindu' comes from the River Sindhu or Indus, in the north-western part of India, a region that is now in Pakistan. When the early Aryans came, there were already people living on the other side of the river. These early settlers – the Indus Valley civilization – together with the Aryans who joined them later, came to be known as 'Hindus'.

"A great discovery was made soon after the First World War by a famous Indian archaeologist, R. D. Banerjee. While he was digging at a place called Harappa in the Indus Valley, Banerjee unearthed the ruins of a civilization that existed around the year 2500 B.C.E. There was evidence that this ancient society used metals and minerals, cultivated the land, grew their own food, reared animals, ate meat and fish, planned their towns and lived in beautiful houses. In addition, they were well versed in music and dance, art and sculpture. They had rules of administration and they worshipped. Hinduism, as we understand it today, has evolved from the beliefs of that ancient civilization of Hindus and Aryans."

"But, Daddy, that civilization existed only in the north-western corner of India. How is it that their ideas about worship spread right through the country and became known as Hinduism?" asked Sikha.

It was Goutam's chance to show off what he knew. With Mr Datta's approval, he began: "The Aryans were worshippers of the forces of Nature. Flashes of lightning, the rolling of thunder, high winds, fire and floods inspired them with awe. When Nature was calm and peaceful, they were happy. They tried to appease the violent side of Nature by worshipping the gods of the sky, wind and earth, and by making sacrifices. They did not make images to worship, and there were no temples – just Nature."

"What about the gods you worship, Goutam?" Anna asked. "And the images I saw at your shrine upstairs?"

Goutam replied confidently, "We are talking about a very long period of time. People started to imagine their gods in many shapes and forms. They created images of gods and goddesses, demons and other creatures out of wood, clay and metal. Later on these figures were kept in specially prepared places. The houses or shelters built for the gods came to be known as temples. In India today you can still see some fine examples of architecture and sculpture in temples which were built several centuries ago.

"An important era started in about 2500 B.C.E. Some sort of literature began to emerge out of the knowledge that people had acquired while they were trying to communicate with Nature and the gods. This literature was called the **Vedas**, as it came from **Vid**, 'knowledge'. According to the Hindus, the Vedas were the utterances of God the Creator heard by the **rishis**, or sages, of ancient times. That is why the other name of the Vedas is **Sruti**, 'heard'. They are the most sacred of the Hindu scriptures.

"Now, coming back to Sikha's question: while the Vedic literature was developing, the Vedic Aryans were also moving further inland. As they advanced they met people whose lives and customs were very different, owing to the varying geographical conditions of the areas where they lived. All these people came under the influence of the Aryans, who were a dominant people, and their religious practices.

"Hinduism in its earliest form began to spread through the

34

Agni, Vedic god of fire

country, but underwent many changes as it blended into the way
of life of these early inhabitants of India. That is why Hindu
customs and practices vary so much from one part of India to
another. It would be narrow to call Hinduism just a religion. It is a
way of life."

35

Mr Datta seemed quite happy with Goutam's explanation.

"So the Hindus comprise many different people," said Anna, "they speak many different languages, follow different life-styles and can even practise their faith in any way they like. What are they looking for, and do they ever find it?"

"You are right, Anna," said Mr Datta, "Hindus can practise their faith in any way they like, but a true Hindu is always searching for Truth. The search is like the conquest of Mount Everest: this became possible because all the successful climbers believed their paths would eventually lead them to the peak of Everest and each followed their own paths with determination and persistent effort. Had they gone round and round the mountainside, taking first one route, then another, Everest would remain unconquered to this day.

"The Truth Hindus strive for is known as **Brahman**, the Ultimate Truth, or God, the Creator. According to the Hindus, there are at least three paths leading to Brahman: the paths of devotion, wisdom and action. If he follows the path of devotion a Hindu learns to love God as his mother, father or friend. While he communicates with God through singing and dancing he loses himself completely in Him. His joy is boundless and he sees God in all beings on earth and loves them all.

"The Hindu who follows the path of wisdom does not limit himself to reading books. He seeks to understand Brahman while, at the same time, trying to understand his own soul, or self, his **Atman**. His aim is to experience God in everything and within himself.

"The path of action is more direct. It simply means a Hindu's total dedication to his work. Thus everyone's work is important and should be carried out with unselfish devotion and with dignity. However, one must not be over-enthusiastic, and risk making mistakes. One has to be cautious because there are punishments and rewards for one's deeds. The good deeds take a Hindu nearer to God while the bad ones push him towards hell.

"These three paths are called the paths of **Yoga** – **Bhakti** (devotion) **Yoga**, **Jnana** (wisdom) **Yoga** and **Karma** (action) **Yoga**. Every Hindu tries to follow them."

Anna called out excitedly, "My friend's elder brother and his wife attend Yoga classes. But they never mentioned all this. I thought they were doing some sort of fitness training!"

"Oh no, Anna," Mr Datta corrected her, "Yoga is much more than physical exercises. It trains the body to assume certain difficult postures called **asanas**. By practising the asanas you control your breathing and gradually you are able to control your mind. You avoid being distracted by other thoughts and calm any restlessness that arises within you. The discipline of Yoga unites your thoughts, feelings and actions. Although the Hindus strive to follow the paths of Yoga in their daily lives, few practise the asanas, because they lack the training needed to take up this strenuous physical activity. That is why, unfortunately, Westerners often interpret the asanas as a form of fitness exercise.

"A Hindu sees the union with Brahman as his ultimate goal in life. When this is achieved his Atman is freed from its earthly bonds. He attains **moksha**, 'release'. If, on the other hand, he does not attain moksha, he is reborn again and again after death. Every time a person is reborn his status at birth is determined by his deeds, or **karma**, during his previous incarnation. As Hindus, we realize the importance of practising our faith. It is only through practice that we can follow the paths leading to God."

No one had noticed when Sikha slipped out of the room. Now she reappeared and announced that lunch was ready.

"What a splendid idea!" said Goutam, and Anna remarked, "I'm always eating when I come here!"

Aspects of Hindu worship

Mr Datta organized the afternoon, saying that after lunch the children would set up the projector, Mrs Datta would show slides of Indian festivals and he would do the washing-up. Mrs Datta tried to protest but the children wouldn't listen. She was, after all, the expert on rituals connected with pujas.

While she showed the slides Mrs Datta explained to Anna that on certain days of the Hindu calendar special pujas are held in honour of Durga, Kali, Lakshmi, Saraswati, Ganesha, Shiva, Krishna and the other deities. In India some of them are celebrated as national festivals. British Hindu communities hold a lot of these special pujas.

"I wish I could take part in one of those colourful festivals," said Anna wistfully, looking at the slides.

"You can always come with us," offered Sikha, "but in India they are really special, and far more fun."

37

"I would certainly like to come," said Anna. "Could you please describe how you perform your pujas? Sikha told me the other day that there are three hundred and thirty million Hindu gods and goddesses. Do you worship them all in the same way? Are there any rules? How do you prepare for the puja?"

"What a lot of questions you ask, Anna!" exclaimed Mrs Datta, delighted by Anna's interest. "This morning Goutam told you about the Vedas. You will find the answers to all your questions in the Vedas. These writings are divided into four parts: the Rig Veda, Sama Veda, Yajur Veda and Atharva Veda. You asked me whether there are any rules of worship. Well, the four Vedas contain hymns to sing and words to say while performing a puja."

"Are the four Vedas very different from one another?"

"Yes. Each deals with a different aspect of worship," replied Mrs Datta. "The ancient Hindus performed a lot of sacrifices, called **yajna**. They would light sacred fires and offer flour, butter, rice, meat and even alcohol to it in order to please the powerful gods of Nature. For each 'sacrifice' they chanted different mantras and performed different rituals.

"Each of the four Vedas contains two major sections: the **Samhita**, 'collection of hymns', and the **Brahmana**, the meaning of the hymns in prose, explaining the purpose of the various rites performed and their importance. The concluding part of the Vedas is called the **Upanishads**. These contain the essence of the Vedas. Their name implies that they are meant to be learned by sitting at the feet of a **guru** or 'teacher'. The **Gita** or **Bhagwat Gita** (the Songs of the Creator) is a holy scripture that developed from the Upanishads."

"The Vedas must be very long if they contain the descriptions of Nature and the gods, and the hymns and procedures," commented Sikha.

Mrs Datta explained that the Samhita and Brahmana sections deal with the major pujas, but the complete Vedas are enormous books. "The Rig Veda alone has nearly eleven thousand verses! The Upanishads are concerned more with 'True Knowledge' or 'Knowledge of God' – Brahman and Atman – than the performance of rites and rituals."

Anna looked puzzled. "I still don't see how ordinary people could understand the Vedas if they were only 'heard' by a few sages," she said.

*North Indian picture of Krishna (the supreme deity in the Bhagwat Gita)
and his consort, Radha*

A scene from the Mahabharata: Arjuna is urged to fight by his charioteer, Krishna.

Goutam responded on behalf of his mother: "I think your problem is the time-scale, Anna. The answer to your question would probably cover a period of a thousand years or more, during which time there were many changes in society and in people's thinking. Wise men wrote handbooks based on the Vedas called **Smriti**, which means 'recollection' or 'what is remembered'. These contained details of rites and rituals, and even of ceremonies that take place within ordinary Hindu households.

"The ancient stories of the **Puranas** also began to appear. The sages based these stories on the lives of different gods and goddesses in order that the teachings of the Vedas would reach the common people in a much simpler and more interesting way."

Mrs Datta said, "I hope at least one of your questions has been answered, Anna. Now you can understand how Hindus like us, who are not scholars of Sanskrit, but people from all walks of life, can practise our faith according to the rules prescribed in our **Shastras** (holy books). There is no Hindu equivalent of the Bible or the Qur'an, but we have several Shastras: the Vedas, the Upanishads, the two great epic poems (the Mahabharata and the

40

Ramayana), the Gita and the Puranas. There are others but these are the main texts. From a very early age the stories of the Mahabharata, the Ramayana and the Puranas are introduced to the children. We have already discussed that. Now let me tell you a bit about our pujas and the deities we choose to worship."

Worship in the home

"When I was a little girl I used to follow my grandmother and my mother when they performed their daily worship," said Mrs Datta. "I helped them pick fresh flowers, and spent hours watching them prepare all the little utensils and offerings. I was fascinated by the way they prayed to the deities, addressing them as living gods. While the devotional songs were sung, and the music played and the bells rang, I used to imagine that the deities actually smiled or moved!

"When I was about eight or nine my mother encouraged me to participate in the puja. I gradually came to know the various ways in which different deities were worshipped. I memorized the hymns and prayers for different occasions and learned how to prepare myself for each one. I observed fasts and understood their significance. Thus, without any special effort or training, simply by following our family traditions, I became familiar with the acts of daily worship and with the **Vratas.**"

"What are they?" asked Anna.

"The Vratas are occasions when fasts are observed and prayers offered in memory of various important events which, according to the Puranas, were supposed to have taken place in heaven and on earth, involving people like us. The gods and goddesses took part in these events, usually in their roles as removers of obstacles and destroyers of evil. A fast held in their honour is said to bring success, cure people suffering from incurable diseases, make the poor rich, help childless couples to have children, and so on.

"Then there are days when special prayers are offered to Vishnu, Shiva, Ganesha, Lakshmi and the other deities. In fact, there are so many rites, ceremonies and celebrations in our religion that there aren't enough days in the calendar to observe them all. That's why we have to choose just a few deities to worship.

"Our choice of deities depends on our family traditions. The gods and goddesses in our family shrine in India have been there for generations. They were inherited by my father from his grandfather and his great-grandfather. It was the same with my husband's family. Lord Lakshmi-Narayan happens to be our **kuladevata** (kula means 'family' and devata means 'deity'). So we worship him in our shrine. None of the others were added for any particular reason. Sometimes you can find relatively modern saints like **Sri Rama Krishna** or **Vivekananda** being worshipped in the family shrine.

"In India the choice also depends on where you live. There may be a guardian deity of the village or the area, a **gramadevata** (grama means 'village' and devata means 'deity'). Some people also like to carry the image of a deity on their person, on a pendant, or set in a ring perhaps. It gives them extra confidence and strength of mind to have their god so close to them. They pray to him whenever they like. This deity is called an **ishtadevata**, or 'personal deity'. He is the one in whom people have the deepest trust.

"A puja is conducted in several stages. It begins with the sounding of a bell. The deities are then addressed, through the images, which are treated with great reverence throughout the puja. This may last a few minutes, an hour or several days. First the feet of the images of the deities are washed, then they are given a bath and a change of clothes and offered food. Finally, the closing prayers are said."

Practising Hinduism in Britain

"I hope you now have some idea of how we perform pujas in our family," said Mrs Datta.

"Yes, thank you," replied Anna. She added, "But, from what I have learned so far, Hinduism seems to be an elaborate affair. Are you able to practise your religion properly in Britain?"

Mrs Datta thought for a moment and answered, "I am not sure what you mean by 'properly'. If you are asking whether we find it difficult to practise our faith, then the answer is both 'Yes' and 'No'. There are practical difficulties, of course: the English climate stops us performing some of the rites and rituals that are often held in the open air. We cannot use water freely in our pujas, either. Pouring water over the gods and goddesses, for example, is not practical here, and the floors cannot be washed with water, for obvious reasons. We can't collect fresh flowers every morning. Dhoob grass, bilwa (wood-apple) leaves and even mangoes, which

42

are important ingredients of the puja, are not readily available because they do not grow in Britain. The bells and the conch cannot be sounded in the same way, nor can hymns be sung in the house, for fear of disturbing the neighbours.

"Family units are small here, so all the pressures of domestic work, jobs and school have to be borne by the parents and children alone, whereas in India, where the extended family is the norm, the responsibilities are shared by other relatives living in the same household. We all leave home fairly early in the morning to get to school or to work and it is usually quite late in the evening when the family gets together again. All this leaves us very little time to perform all the rites of our daily worship as required by our religious tradition.

"On those occasions when a puja is held on a much larger scale, a very important aspect of it – the immersion ceremony – cannot be performed according to our Shastras because the images cannot be carried through the streets to be cast into the river. Yes, there are many problems. In Britain the pace of life is fast and there are far too many commitments to fulfil. We are so busy working for material success and coping with the pressures of daily living that

Ornate platforms on which deities are carried in procession, Orissa

Hindu families celebrating Dussera in Victoria Park, Finchley

we leave ourselves little time to think of God or 'recharge our batteries'. But if we can rise above all this and look at the situation from a religious angle, our minds filled with the happiness of prayer and thoughts of God the Creator, we see many positive signs.

"Take some simple examples: the food available in Britain used to pose problems for Hindus, but nowadays people have become aware of each other's needs and shops and supermarkets can usually cater for every religious community. Most of the ingredients required to perform a puja are now available. There are also many Hindu temples and centres where the community may worship together, and where religious seminars are held on a regular basis. There are priests who visit families to conduct family pujas and ceremonies. Discussions are held in schools on world religions. Children want to know more about the backgrounds of their friends from different parts of the world. These are all very encouraging signs.

"So, all I can say is that I am able to practise my faith with a clear conscience in spite of the difficulties. I feel that our religion is broad enough to make allowances for any lapses on our part. One must, however, make every effort to keep within the limits prescribed by our holy texts while worshipping either at home or in a communal place. One must not take liberties in the name of religion. The most important thing is to practise."

44

5
Temples

Mr Datta's brother had stopped in London for a week on his way
to Boston. At Sikha's request he had brought a miniature of the
famous Jagannath Temple for Anna. It was a beautiful model
carved out of soapstone by some of the finest craftsmen in India.
Like the temple itself, it was made in four sections, each one a
complete building. When placed on a polished wooden base it
looked very like the actual gigantic structure which has been
standing on its own grounds in the town of Puri for centuries.

Goutam arranged the model on the coffee-table. They all sat
round to look at it more closely and admired the delicate carvings
on its walls. There were the most elaborate and intricate patterns
of leaves, flowers and creepers, of birds and animals and people.

Anna had never seen anything like it. She gasped in amazement
when Mrs Datta said, "This is for you, Anna, a belated birthday
present from all of us."

"Oh no!" Anna was so overcome by emotion that she couldn't
say any more. She simply rushed over to Mrs Datta, embraced her
and said, "Thank you very much. You are all so kind!"

Mr Datta smiled and said, "If this is how you feel looking at a
model, I wonder what might happen if you were to stand in front
of the real temple! It is a majestic structure, but sadly, much
neglected these days. It is probably the most famous temple in the
State of Orissa because it houses **Lord Jagannath**, the guardian
deity of the province. You will come across temples wherever you
go in India, large ones and small ones, some very old and famous
and others fairly modern. It is obvious that a temple is a place of
worship, housing a certain god or goddess or even a number of
deities. But, in fact, a temple is much more than that. In order to
understand all the functions of our temples it often helps to know
the legends connected with them."

45

Entrance to the Jagannath Temple, Puri

"Well," said Anna, "now that I have just acquired this precious gift, I think I ought to know a little about its history."

"You are absolutely right," Mr Datta agreed, "but before I say • any more, take another good look at the model. The temple at Puri was built over eight hundred years ago and is nearly sixty metres tall. It covers a vast area of ground. Its outer walls and the whole of the interior are lavishly decorated with a variety of sculpture. Then there are the other buildings around the main temple, each built for a different purpose.

"Imagine how long it must have taken to build a structure like this without the aid of modern technology! How many people must have worked on it, and how expensive it must have been! Now, can you tell me who could have undertaken such a mammoth task?"

Without any hesitation Anna said, "Only kings or rulers could have done it, because they had the royal treasury at their disposal and could employ as many people as they pleased."

"You get full marks for that!" cried Mr Datta. "Let me tell you who it was that built this masterpiece. The story goes that a very long time ago there was a mighty king named Indradyumna. He wanted to build a temple that would outclass all the rest in size and beauty. It was to serve as a monument to remind his people of him after his death. Indradyumna had a vision in which he saw Lord Nilamadhava, a form of Jagannath (literally, 'Lord of the Universe'), who is an incarnation of Vishnu. Lord Nilamadhava dwelt in an obscure cave and was worshipped every day by the chief of a tribe known as the Sabaras.

"Indradyumna decided that this was the deity for his proposed temple since the Lord himself had revealed his intentions through the vision. For many days his officers searched far and wide for the deity until Vidyapati, the youngest and the most enterprising of them all, came across the chief of the Sabaras in a remote forest region. He spent a long time with him, won his confidence and married his daughter. She later told him where the deity was.

"Vidyapati stole the image of Lord Nilamadhava and brought it to the king. The Sabara chief, Viswavasu, was so grief-stricken at the loss of his favourite deity that he wanted to end his life. Lord Nilamadhava took pity on his devotee and left the king by vanishing mysteriously from the palace. The king was bewildered by the deity's disappearance and he too was overcome by grief.

"Then King Indradyumna heard a heavenly voice asking him to build a temple for his favourite god. When this was done he was to retrieve a floating log at the seashore. The new image of the deity would be carved out of this log and would be known as Lord Jagannath. However, the king would not be able to carry the log to the temple without the help of Viswavasu, the Sabara chief. Thus Lord Nilamadhava brought about a reconciliation between his two great devotees, Indradyumna and Viswavasu."

Sikha took up the story: "Indradyumna asked the architect god **Viswakarma** to carve the statue for him. Viswakarma said he would, on condition that he was allowed to complete the work behind closed doors, unseen by anyone. The king agreed, but after a while his curiosity got the better of him and he peeped into the temple to see how the sculpture was progressing. Furious,

Viswakarma stormed off, leaving the image unfinished, without hands or feet!"

"Some say it was the queen who peeped in," interrupted Goutam, "but there are different versions of most folk-tales."

"Anyway," continued Sikha, "Indradyumna begged forgiveness for his foolish action, and Lord Brahma took pity on him. He infused the statue with godly powers, even though it wasn't complete, and for centuries the temple of Lord Jagannath has been visited by millions of people from all over the world every year."

"You may be interested to know that the word 'Juggernaut' is connected with the worship of Jagannath," said Mr Datta, turning to Anna. "English people use the word to refer to huge trains or lorries that run people over. It can also mean a monstrous system or giant organization that crushes people, in a figurative sense. However, the real Juggernauts are three enormous wooden chariots in which the images of Lord Jagannath, his brother Balabhadra and their sister Subhadra are placed. The chariots are nearly fourteen metres high and their wheels are over two metres in diameter. Every year in Puri, at the festival of **Rath Yatra** (the Car Festival), thousands of devotees pull the chariots along. In their enthusiasm to earn the blessings of the deities, many get carried away, and some fall under the giant wheels.

Statuettes of Jagannath, Balabhadra and Subhadra

48

Rath Yatra in Trafalgar Square

"We went to the Rath Yatra celebrations in Trafalgar Square last year, and saw the three chariots that had been built to carry the deities. It was a very colourful celebration. Thousands of people were there, but luckily no one was run over by the chariots!

"Returning to the subject of temples," went on Mr Datta, "the architecture of the temple and its sculptural decorations tell us a lot about the time when it was built. There are detailed carvings of scenes from the great epics – the Ramayana and the Mahabharata – and scenes from real events of the time, such as coronations, military victories, royal weddings and processions. The sculptors and craftsmen were instructed by their patrons to illustrate historical events on temple walls so that the people would see the similarity between the lives of their rulers and those of the gods and goddesses."

Anna remembered the conversation she had with Sikha during her first visit to the Dattas' house. "Now I can see what Sikha meant when she said Hindu deities are like real people, but people who can influence the lives of ordinary human beings," she said.

"That's true," replied Mr Datta. "By creating such realistic images, the great sculptors brought the stories about the deities to life. The fact that the carvings appeared on the very walls of the 'houses of the gods' made the stories even more convincing."

Mrs Datta had several chores to attend to. She left the rest of them to continue their discussion.

"Were there any other reasons for building temples?" Sikha asked her father.

Mr Datta said, "Some of the temples were built by a ruler or a patron to mark an important event connected with their reign or one that took place in their lifetime. For example, a victory in battle which they believed was achieved through God's help, or a wedding or birth in the family which had great political significance and was seen as a blessing from God.

"A ruler could command the respect of his subjects in two ways: first, by his ability to protect his people; and secondly, through his benevolence as the servant of his people. One of the ways a ruler could show his generosity was by building a temple where his subjects could worship."

"I expect the craftsmen enjoyed a lot of privileges."

"Oh, absolutely!" Mr Datta replied. "They were famous people

Carvings on a temple gateway

whose reputation spread from one end of the kingdom to the other, and beyond. They enjoyed the royal favours showered on them in the form of money, land, titles and, above all, prestige. The temple became the focus of attention of every section of the community, so it had to be grand and impressive, and the great sculptors went out of their way to beautify the temple walls. To the people, the king was next to God Himself! It was he who had created the magnificent temple in order to bring God nearer to his people. Here they could stand in His presence and worship.

"The decorations on the walls contributed a lot to the development of education, too. They covered themes ranging from nature and religion to politics and helped people to appreciate this form of art which, in the course of time, influenced the music and dance of India."

"Really! How?" asked Anna.

Mr Datta smiled and said, "I wish I could take you to the real temple of Lord Jagannath right now! Then you could look closely at the carvings, and touch them too, and you would appreciate just how delicate and graceful their features are. This model is far too small for that."

Sikha seemed to remember something suddenly and left the room saying, "Just a minute!" She returned with a beautiful statue of a woman preening herself in front of a mirror. This was a miniature from the temple sculpture in the Dattas' display cabinet.

"Well done!" cried Mr Datta. "I had completely forgotten about it!"

"What a beautiful figure!" Anna exclaimed.

"Isn't it life-like? Look," said Mr Datta, "you can almost see the movement of her hand. It makes you peep into the mirror to see the reflection. Look at her relaxed posture, the proportion of her limbs, her balance and grace! In fact, it is so true to life that you feel as if the lady might turn round and walk away!

"Now, in the classical Indian dances, the performers try to capture the many moods expressed by the figures created by those great sculptors. The dancers have to undergo a rigorous process of training in order to master all the postures. It may take a lifetime."

"Is there a fixed number of positions to learn?"

"The answer is both 'Yes' and 'No'," said Mr Datta. "There are one hundred and eight basic and thirty-two advanced poses, but the subject is as vast as life itself. All our moods and expressions

51

Tenth-century statue from a temple in Bhubaneswar, Orissa

can hardly be contained within that prescribed number. Therefore, in order to express other feelings a dancer has to improvise. The more talented the dancer, the finer and more expressive are the gestures. The greatest of all dancers is Lord Shiva himself. He is called **Nataraja**, or the King of all Dancers."

Anna seemed very taken by the temple sculptures. She kept turning the statue over to look at it from all angles. After a while she put it down carefully and returned to the model of the temple.

"In which of the four buildings of the temple is the statue of Lord Jagannath installed?" she asked. "And what happens in the other sections?"

Nataraja: Shiva as Lord of Dance

"Before I answer your questions," said Mr Datta, "let me tell you a bit about some of the ideas behind temple building. I am not an architect, but I learned quite a lot from the old priests at the temple of Lord Jagannath. Mountains are sacred to all Hindus. In our mythology, Kailasa is the most sacred of all the mountains, because it is the home of **Mahadeva** (another name for Shiva). Caves, too, are considered to be sacred, since they have been the dwelling-place of many gods. That is why the ancient architects designed temples to resemble mountain peaks. The highest point of a temple is called 'sikhara', the summit. This part is always in line with the very core, the centre of the building, where the deity is installed.

"Therefore, in your model, Anna, the highest of the four temple buildings is the main temple, housing Lord Jagannath. As you enter this building you gradually approach its deepest and darkest, cave-like part. It becomes very narrow and there is very little natural light. In some temples, you will have to go down several deep steps to reach the level where the deity is. As you stand here and look at the massive walls around you and the enormous dome-shaped ceiling above your head, you feel as though you are inside an underground cavern and in the presence of God. This area is called 'garbha-griha', the 'womb' of the temple.

"The other buildings serve several different purposes. The ones leading up to the main temple are the 'gateway', which is very elaborate, and the 'hallways' where there are other gods and goddesses. The devotees usually congregate here before reaching the small chamber to offer their prayers to the deity.

"Somewhere, either at the gateway or at the second stage, under the arch leading to the hall, there is a bell. This is rung once by each of the devotees as they enter the temple."

"Why?" asked Anna.

Mr Datta raised his eyebrows. "What a question! Why, don't you ring the doorbell when you visit someone?"

"Oh yes! Of course!" Anna blushed. "I wasn't thinking." Everyone laughed.

Mr Datta went on: "Depending on the size of the temple, there may be annexes and outhouses, a tank for bathing, wells, gardens and living-quarters, all in the same compound. There may be schools for studying Sanskrit, elementary schools, classes for music and dance, a library, shops and even banks and post offices.

A temple is very much at the centre of the community which it serves in so many ways."

Anna thanked him for telling her about Hindu temples in India. Pointing to the model on the table, she added, "Is there a temple like this one in Britain?"

Mr Datta replied "No, Anna. We have a number of Hindu temples in Britain, but none like that. Can anyone guess why? You should know the answer by now."

Goutam nodded and said, "Temples like this were built in India centuries ago, whereas there were no Hindu temples in Britain until the sixties. But let us look at some English cathedrals of England built between the eleventh and fifteenth centuries. Canterbury Cathedral is one of the oldest. Work first started here in the eleventh century. Then there is the great York Minster, built in the thirteenth century. These two magnificent buildings still stand, drawing vast numbers of people from all over the world and earning their admiration. Yet what happens when they are damaged or destroyed, like the fourteenth century cathedral at Coventry, for instance?" Goutam paused and asked, "Have you seen the new Coventry Cathedral, Anna?"

"No, not yet. Why?" she replied and hastily added, "I have been to Canterbury Cathedral, though."

"Well, the original Coventry Cathedral was destroyed during the war and the great architect Sir Basil Spence designed and completed the new, giant cathedral in 1962. It is imposing and very impressive, but somehow I can't accept it. Because I am accustomed to those old, historic temples of India, I felt at home when I visited the cathedrals of Canterbury and York, but Coventry Cathedral did not have the same effect on me. I felt very sad to visit the ruins of the old cathedral on which the new one stands."

Mr Datta smiled. "Goutam is rather biased, you know," he said, although he did not disagree with his son's views. He had felt the same!

"So, as you can see," continued Mr Datta, "a temple like this could not be built today because we don't have the resources to build it. There are no Hindu kings living in Britain who would be prepared to undertake such a task. But then, not all Hindu temples are of the same stature – there are small ones, too. Think of all the village shrines tucked away under the trees! Let us lower our sights a bit and find out how present-day Hindu temples began to appear in Britain. I have already told you how the ancient temple became a centre for the community it served, haven't I?"

"Yes," answered Anna and Sikha.

"When I arrived here," said Mr Datta, "there were no such places. In the early sixties I used to feel very restless, especially on festival days. I pined for the company of other Hindus with whom I might share my thoughts and feelings. Fortunately, there were many others who felt the same. Some were prominent members of the local Hindu community, and they eventually got together and formed the Hindu Centre in London in 1962."

"Is that the name of the temple?" asked Anna.

Mr Datta replied, "It is not a temple as such. It is an association – a cultural and social centre. It doesn't look like a temple, either. It is a large terraced house with an adjoining hall which was purchased with the help of donations in 1968. There is a resident priest and a shrine with Lord Krishna as the main deity. The satsang, or 'meeting', of the devotees and their friends takes place on the first Sunday of every month."

Evening puja being offered by an International Society of Krishna Consciousness priest on a special occasion at Hatch End School, Middlesex

"I see!" Anna commented. "The Centre is based on the same principles as the Hindu temples in India, but it is funded through donations rather than royal patronage."

"That is correct," said Mr Datta. "It also conducts marriages, sacred-thread ceremonies, cremation pujas and other ceremonies. At the satsang assemblies important events in the Hindu calendar are celebrated: Dussera, Holi, Divali, Vasant Panchami and Saraswati Puja, the birthdays of Lord Krishna, Rama and so on. A cultural programme of talks, music and dance followed by **preeti bhojan,** a communal feast hosted by a member, are usually a part of such celebrations. There is a library, a reading-room and an assembly hall, which can be hired out for community functions."

"So Hindu temples in Britain are all in converted houses or churches and were not specially built."

"Yes, as far as I know," replied Mr Datta. "While the Hindu Centre was moving into its own premises in London, another Hindu society was forming: the Hindu Cultural Society of Bradford. Again, between 1964 and 1965 a small group was formed in someone's house in Coventry. This association was later called the Hindu Satsang Mandal. In due course it set up the Shree Krishna Temple. Here, besides their main deities, Lord Krishna and Radha, they also worship Lord Ganesha."

"I had no idea there were so many Hindu temples in Britain."

"There is in fact a body called the National Council of Hindu Temples (U.K.) which lists about thirty such associations as affiliated members, and there are bound to be a few more that are not members."

"And each one of them has its own story," remarked Anna, "although I shouldn't think any of them is as touching or dramatic as the story of King Indradyumna and Vidyapati."

Mr Datta sighed, "You are absolutely right, Anna. The modern legends connected with Hindu temples only tell us about mundane things like planning permission, town councils and problems with finance. However, they also describe the struggles of communities determined to set up a temple, the generosity of the donors and the great efforts by individuals to create a venue where the religious and cultural life of Hindus may be enriched."

Anna picked up the model again. "I wish I could see a deity being worshipped in a real temple like this," she said.

Mrs Datta overheard Anna's remark as she came into the lounge carrying her usual tray of home-made goodies. "Even a belated birthday present is never complete without a little misti-mookh," she said, smiling. "'Misti-mookh' is a Bengali name meaning 'sweet mouth', something sweet to eat," she explained.

Everyone welcomed the arrival of the tray, especially Mr Datta, when he saw the steaming cups of tea – he was very thirsty from so much talking!

"Why not visit the Shree Ganapathy Temple at Wimbledon this weekend?" suggested Mrs Datta.

Mr Datta choked and coughed. He had just taken a sip of tea. Recovering quickly, he apologized, saying, "I'm so sorry. ... Why didn't I think of that? Of course we could go there!"

This unexpected development made Anna suspicious. "Well, what is so special about that temple?" she asked.

Mrs Datta replied, "The temple of Shree Ganapathy is perhaps the most recent of all the Hindu temples in Britain. It is only four years old! Although it is also a converted Presbyterian church building and nothing like the Jagannath Temple, the story of its growth matches, to some extent, the ones about our ancient temples."

"Please explain," Anna pleaded.

"This temple grew very swiftly, due to the determination, dedication and devotion of a number of devotees," began Mrs Datta. "Among them were builders, decorators and electricians who worked day and night to convert the church into a Hindu temple. Even children worked there, as hard as their parents, throughout their summer holiday. From all over Europe devotees flocked to offer their services.

"As you enter the temple you can feel the atmosphere. The traditional rules of temple building have been observed. On entering the temple you proceed to the deepest section of the building, where a large statue of **Lord Ganapathy** (or **Ganapati** – Ganesha) is installed in the inner sanctum. The image was created by the sculptors of Mahabalipuram in South India. The highest part of the temple, known as the Gopuram, rises in the shape of a dome above the seat of the Lord. Facing the main deity, on a raised dais, there is a statue of the 'great mouse' – the Lord's mount – looking up at its master. All around the main deity there are several other deities, standing on their respective platforms in the hall and in the niches in the wall, just as you would see them in our ancient temples.

At the Shree Ganapathy Temple, Wimbledon, a devotee exposes her palms to the flames of the lamp.

"On a warm day the resident priest stands in front of the altar barefooted and bare-bodied, wearing only his saffron-coloured lower garment wrapped round his waist and his sacred thread across his shoulder. While he chants Sanskrit hymns, families of devotees come in, bringing offerings of flowers, fruit, sweetmeats, etc. They stand silently, their arms folded, as the priest performs the puja. At the end the priest holds the five-branched **arati** lamp up to the devotees. They warm their palms over its flames and touch their own heads and those of their children who cannot reach the lamp themselves. This gesture symbolizes sharing the warmth with the deity and receiving the blessings. The priest then gives them a spoonful of holy water called **Charanamrita** to sip."

"It sounds wonderful!" said Anna excitedly.

Mrs Datta continued, "In the adjoining hall regular classes are held for music, dance and religious discussions. There is even extra tuition for sixth-form pupils, in science subjects and maths. ... Yes, it is important to visit a temple. The atmosphere helps to concentrate your mind on your prayer. You are not distracted by other thoughts. God is everywhere, of course, and there are those who can pray anywhere, not just in temples, but ordinary people like us may not often rise to their level. Lord Krishna said, 'I am in every religion as the thread through a string of pearls. Wherever thou seest extraordinary holiness and extraordinary power and purifying humanity, know thou that I am there.'"

59

6
Rakhi Purnima

The summer holiday had just started but Anna was already getting bored at home. Suddenly the telephone rang. It was Sikha, asking her if she would like to go shopping. She was going to Southall to get some **Rakhis**.

"What are they?" asked Anna.

"They're beautiful amulets, made from pieces of mica, cork, tinsel and silk. You tie them on people's wrists on special occasions," said Sikha.

"That sounds interesting. You'll have to tell me more when we meet." Anna put the receiver down and rushed upstairs to get ready.

On the way to Southall, Sikha told Anna that on **Purnima**, the full-moon day in the month of Shravana, which is the fourth month of the Hindu calendar, a special ceremony takes place. Sisters tie Rakhis on their brothers' wrists for luck and for protection against evil influences. Every brother considers this gesture a great honour and promises to act as his sister's protector. A woman sometimes gives a friend the status of a brother by tying a Rakhi on his wrist on Purnima. Rakhis are also sent by post to people who are far away from home.

"Do you know how the custom began?" Anna asked her friend.

"Yes, according to the Puranas, **Indra** (the leader of the gods) once lost his kingdom to the asuras (demons) in a war. He desperately wanted to regain his kingdom and regrouped his army. Just before he set out for the battlefield his wife tied a Rakhi on his wrist to wish him luck. Indra conquered the demons and won back his kingdom."

Sikha added that on Purnima in India the Brahmins go around visiting the families for whom they act as priests and tie Rakhis on the wrists of their clients. While they do this they sing hymns of

Rakhis

blessing. In return they receive a gift, which is usually money. This occasion is called **Rakhi Purnima** in some parts of the country. It is also the day when the Brahmins change their **Upavita**, the sacred thread they wear across their shoulders, in a ceremony called "Raksha Bandhan". Raksha means "Rakhi" and Bandhan is the Sanskrit word for "tying".

"Obviously, you are going to get a Rakhi for Goutam. Do you think I could give him one too?" Anna asked shyly.

"Of course you can. He would be delighted!" Sikha was thrilled.

She was quite right. Goutam felt very honoured when both Anna and Sikha tied a Rakhi on his wrist. By tradition, he was expected to give them some money in return, but he decided to thank them by taking them to the cinema instead.

QUESTIONS AND PROJECTS
Chapters 4–6

1   What is the moral of the story about Gopal in Chapter 4?

2   Draw a map of the Indian subcontinent to show the principal cities (Delhi, Calcutta, Madras and Bombay). Add the Ganges, Indus, Mahanadi and Godavari rivers and the holy cities along the Ganges (Hardwar, Varanashi (Benares), Patna, etc.).

3   Write an account of one episode in the history of the British in India.

4   Write a short story using the title "Children of God".

5   Talk to people you know who practise Yoga. Do they see it as a mental or spiritual discipline, or as a form of physical training?

6   The Ramayana and the Mahabharata contain many good stories. Choose one story from either and tell it in your own words. You could also act it out as a short play or paint a picture to illustrate it.

7   Study some statues or carvings of deities worshipped by primitive or ancient societies. Make a model of one such figure. Why do you think people create images representing supernatural, powerful beings?

8   Give examples of buildings or monuments decorated with sculpture commemorating events in British history. You will probably find at least one in your own area.

9   If possible, arrange a visit to a Hindu temple. The Hindu Centre (see p.158) may be able to supply the address of the one nearest you. After your visit, draw a plan of the temple and make notes to show how the different areas are used.

10 Try to visit Trafalgar Square for the Rath Yatra celebrations. Don't forget to take a camera!

11 Write a story based on the spirit of Rakhi Purnima.

7
Dress

Anna stood in front of the mirror holding the end of the sari which was to go over her shoulder while Sikha adjusted the pleats.

"You have done it very well," Sikha congratulated her. "It takes a while to learn how to gather these pleats, but it gets easier with practice."

"Thanks," said Anna. "I was worried that the sari would look untidy or start to come off!"

While the two friends were adjusting the sari Mrs Datta walked into the room. She was wearing a pure white cotton sari with an extra-wide border of bright red. It had no pleats. She had wound about half the sari round her waist. The other half went over her left shoulder, then over her head and back over her shoulder. A big bunch of keys was tied to one end of the sari. A most unusual style! Mrs Datta's hair was loose, hanging almost to her hips and covering her back. There was a bright line of vermilion along the parting in her hair and a large vermilion dot between her eyebrows.

"You look so different, Mrs Datta," Anna said, smiling, "but very nice. I didn't realize you had such long hair."

"Yes, what a surprise, Mummy!" agreed Sikha. "For a moment I thought we were in India!" She giggled. "The bunch of keys goes well with your sari, but it does look a bit out of place over here, doesn't it? Are you performing a puja?"

"No, there is no puja today," replied her mother, "but Anna was asking about traditional Indian dress the other day. As this is a typically Hindu style, I thought it would be a suitable one to demonstrate." Looking at Anna, she asked, "Well, what do you think?"

"I think it's lovely, but I have never seen anyone wearing a sari like that," answered Anna.

63

Hindu women wearing saris at a festival in London

Here the sari is worn without a choli (Bengal, about 1950).

"British Hindus don't usually wear this style," Sikha explained, "but it is how the typical Bengali housewife and mother wears her sari. I suppose its simplicity – the lack of pleats, for example – shows that the style came from the country. My grandmother does not always wear a **choli** – a blouse or bodice – but she uses more than half of her sari to wrap round her head and the upper part of her body."

"Why did you ask if there was a puja?" enquired Anna.

"Well, this is the first time Mummy has dressed like this since we came to live in London, but I didn't realize that she had done it just to show you. In India she used to look like this every morning after her bath as she prepared for the daily worship at our family shrine."

Mrs Datta smiled and said, "That is true, Anna. It was my daily routine. Today my hair is not wet, but in India after a bath the hair is allowed to dry like this, naturally. Hardly anyone uses hair-driers. The vermilion in the parting of my hair shows that I am a married person and my husband is alive. It was put on on the day of my marriage. A wife will wear it with great pride all her married life. The large red dot of vermilion is really a decoration and is also popular with young girls. They may use a paint called **kumkum** instead of vermilion. You can also buy small coloured plastic counters which are simply stuck on.

"I should remind you that what I'm wearing is the traditional dress of a Hindu housewife only in Bengal. In India, styles of dress vary so much from one region to another that it is virtually impossible to call any one of them typically Hindu."

"Is it the same for men's clothes?" asked Anna.

"Yes, the same rule applies. Styles vary from province to province and you cannot say that any one of them is typically Hindu."

"Yes, you can, Mummy!" put in Sikha. "What about the holy men?"

Mrs Datta laughed and said, "You are right, I suppose. Holy men, especially the elderly ones, are usually bearded with long hair. Their clothing varies from the scantiest loincloth to flowing robes of saffron or white. They often have a mark on their forehead called **Tilak**. This shows which deity they follow. A lot of holy men, particularly the followers of Shiva, smear their bodies with ash. Their appearance gives the impression of renunciation

65

A wandering holy man

and self-sacrifice. Such people follow a religious path in preference
to any other occupation or vocation. They will often lessen their
ties with their own families and spend most of their time in pursuit
of God and Truth. Holy men are unique in that sense. Naturally,
ordinary people do not dress like them."

"I understand," said Anna. "Another thing: while watching
crowd scenes filmed in India on television I have noticed that a
large number of men wear trousers and shirts, like Western
summer clothes. Almost all the boys wear shorts, too. Is that the
normal practice?"

"Yes," replied Mrs Datta. "Most boys prefer shorts, even in
the villages, and trousers and shirts are popular with students,
teachers and office-workers. In this regard the West has influenced
men's fashions since the days of the Raj. But the true Indian dress
for men is the dhoti, of course, although hardly anyone wears a
dhoti in Britain."

"Why is that?" enquired Anna.

"Well, the dhoti is not suitable for outdoor wear in this country.
Although, like the sari, it is a single piece of cloth about six metres
long and a metre wide, the way it is tied round the waist does not
allow room for a warm undergarment, and dhotis are made from
lightweight material," explained Mrs Datta. "You cannot wear a
petticoat under a dhoti as you can with a sari."

Rice-paddy being trampled by bullocks. Note the farmer's turban and short dhoti.

Sikha giggled at the thought of her father wearing a petticoat underneath his dhoti!

Mrs Datta continued, "The dhoti is worn in many different ways. It is usually white and made of cotton, but in north-western areas of India silk and coloured dhotis are sometimes worn by the bridegroom, the priest and others taking part in a wedding."

"Isn't it hard to move in such a long piece of material?"

"Yes, it is, to some extent. That is the reason why a lot of people, young and old, have adopted shorts and trousers in preference to the dhoti. In the villages, however, you will see farmers working quite easily with their dhoti pulled up above their knees and drawn through their legs to serve as shorts or baggy trousers."

"Do only poor men wear a dhoti?"

"Not really," said Mrs Datta. "You see, it comes in a variety of materials. The coarser, narrower dhotis are preferred by village people because they last longer and are comparatively cheap. But there are expensive ones, made of superfine material. These are worn in elegant style under the kurta, or tunic. A shawl may also be worn in cold weather. In the summer months, particularly in the south where the winters are mild and the atmosphere humid, many men often do not bother to cover the upper part of their bodies. They also walk barefooted. There is something else you

67

may have noticed," she added. "Some men shave their heads, leaving a tuft of hair at the back. This is called the **Choti** or **Tikee**. It is another sign of belonging to a particular religious group. Such men are **Vaishnavs** – followers of Vishnu, of whom Krishna is an incarnation."

"Hindu men also wear a sacred thread, the Upavita, don't they, Mummy?" said Sikha.

"Not all of them do. Your father doesn't, nor does Goutam. It is not strictly required in our caste, but for the Brahmins it is compulsory."

"What exactly is a sacred thread?" Anna asked.

Mrs Datta explained, "It is a piece of cotton thread made up of three strands woven together, each of which is itself made up of three strands. At a ceremony of initiation called **Upanayana**, conducted by a priest, the length of thread is put on the left shoulder of each boy and passed across his body. The ends are tied in a sacred knot under his right arm. Afterwards, the Gayatri, the most sacred verses in the Rig Veda, are whispered into the boy's ear and he has to repeat them. All Brahmins wearing a sacred thread are expected to memorize the Gayatri. The thread is never discarded, although it is changed when it wears out."

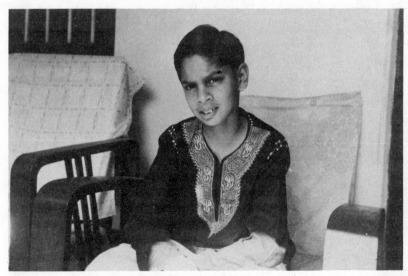

Young boy in a beautifully embroidered kurta

"I have never seen anyone wearing a sacred thread," Anna remarked.

"I don't think you will in Britain, unless you attend a religious ceremony conducted in an orthodox manner, where the priest and those taking part leave the upper part of their body uncovered," said Mrs Datta. "The sacred thread is worn next to the body, under a vest, you see. Although the Upavita is a part of Hindu dress with a religious significance, it is not worn by all Hindus, and it isn't as obvious as a tie or a turban."

"I thought only Sikhs wore turbans."

"No, some Hindus wear them too," replied Mrs Datta. "For some Hindus the turban is part of their traditional dress. Villagers, particularly farmers working in the fields, wear turbans to protect their heads from the scorching heat of the sun. According to certain customs a turban is worn by a bridegroom as a part of his wedding outfit, particularly in the northern and north-western parts of India. In southern and south-eastern areas, the bridegroom wears an elaborate wedding-hat made of pith. It is decorated with cut-out and carved patterns. In North India a lot of Hindus prefer to wear caps, but these are not so popular in the south-eastern regions, particularly Assam, Bengal, Orissa and all along the eastern coast. The turbans and other headgear worn by Hindus don't necessarily have any religious significance. Sometimes they indicate the wearer's occupation or birthplace."

"Again, I haven't seen many Hindus with turbans, either," said Anna.

"That's true," agreed Mrs Datta. "In Britain, turbans are not everyday wear for modern Hindus. They are used on ceremonial occasions and only by certain communities. The only people who wear turbans in Britain are the Sikhs, for whom it is a religious requirement, whether they wear Western or traditional Indian dress. Their turbans are very smart."

Anna tried to sum up what she had learned. "From what you have been saying," she began, "it seems that although there are so many variations in the way Hindus dress, the dhoti and the kurta are probably the most common garments for men, and the sari and the choli for women."

"That's right," said Mrs Datta. She added, "There are two other types of garment which are also popular among Hindus. One of them is called a 'ghagra' and is seen in North India. It is a very full

69

pleated skirt. The upper garment consists of a choli and a dupatta, which is like a stole and covers the head and the shoulders. The other style is a long tunic called a 'kameez' or kurta, which is worn over trousers. This is basically a Muslim style of dress, but because of its elegance it has become very popular with young ladies. But the sari has always dominated the scene."

"The sari is my favourite," said Anna. "There are so many different kinds of saris and people wear them in so many different ways."

"What different styles have you noticed?" asked Mrs Datta with a smile.

"Well," Anna began slowly, "elderly women wear their sari in a baggy style, without pleats at the front. The effect is very different to yours, of course, Mrs Datta! Almost all of them cover their heads with the end of their sari. Many wear a completely white borderless sari with a white choli. Am I right?" Anna asked anxiously.

"Absolutely!" Mrs Datta encouraged her. "The ladies you describe are mostly Hindu women from the western state of Gujarat. Some of those wearing a plain white sari have probably lost their husbands, since this way of dressing symbolizes widowhood. Widows do not have the red vermilion mark in the parting of their hair, either. What have you noticed about the younger or more fashionable women?"

Anna thought for a while, then answered, "The ones I see in London generally wear chiffon or nylon saris, printed or embroidered with different patterns. The sari is pleated at the front, then goes round the back. The rest is gathered over the shoulder and falls down to cover the back. Underneath they wear a short-sleeved bodice; if it's warm enough, a few wear a sleeveless one."

"That is perfect," exclaimed Mrs Datta. "Lightweight synthetic materials are preferred because they are easy to wash, need very little ironing and dry quickly, and that's very helpful in this climate! However, in order to appreciate why a Hindu girl feels so strongly about her sari you have to understand our custom.

"A sari is a symbol of maturity. Once a girl has discarded the dresses she wears as a child and has changed over to a sari, she has, in a way, proclaimed her adulthood. As she grows into a woman and her wedding-day approaches, her parents give her the most

70

beautiful sari she will ever have. It is red — because red is the auspicious colour for a bride — and is made of silk, with elaborate patterns and borders in gold and silver brocade.

"The makers of these saris specialize in many different styles. Among the most famous are the Kanchivaram sari of the South, the Kashmiri Sari, and the Benareshi or Varanashi sari of the North. Such saris are very expensive. For daily wear people prefer cool cotton saris."

"Indian women wear beautiful jewellery, too," added Sikha.

"Yes," agreed Mrs Datta. "From the earliest times both Hindu men and women have loved to wear ornaments, as we can see from temple carvings and paintings, which show even the gods and goddesses decked with jewellery. The descriptions of the goddess Saraswati and Sita, wife of Lord Rama, suggest that they adorned themselves with many fine ornaments of gold and silver and wore pearl necklaces. The very prestigious piece of jewellery called 'Vaijayanti', a special decoration worn by Hindu brides today, is named after the necklace of Lord Vishnu. The most beautiful description of ornaments worn by both human and divine characters is probably found in the verses composed by the great poet Kalidasa of the fifth century.

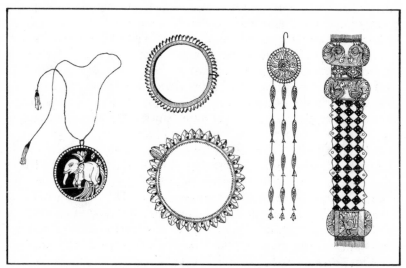

A pendant, two bracelets, a hairpin and a section of a belt, all of silver

71

"Nature is well represented in the patterns and styles of our jewellery. Craftsmen painstakingly reproduce the lotus flower, the conch shell, the peacock and the swan, the snake and the fish, the elephant, leaves and creepers and many holy symbols while designing some of the daintiest and most valuable ornaments in the world. The jewellery worn by the daughter of a wealthy Hindu on her wedding-day will display all these designs. Yes, the Hindus – especially the women – wear jewellery from head to toe, on their head, ears, nose, neck, arms, wrists, hands, waist, ankles and toes."

Anna looked puzzled. "But over here Hindus wear hardly any jewellery!"

Mrs Datta smiled and looked at her daughter. Sikha picked up the newspaper and pointed to a report of a mugging incident. Anna could see her point.

Mrs Datta continued, "Society has become too violent, not just in Britain, but everywhere in the world. Very few women would like to lose their precious belongings in this way, so they wear only imitation jewellery and keep the rest in the bank."

"It is a shame, isn't it?" said Sikha. "We haven't mentioned hairstyles yet," she reminded her mother.

"Ah, hairstyles," began Mrs Datta. "I've already mentioned the tuft of hair that some men wear. Among the women long and glossy black hair is admired by all. To encourage her hair to grow a Hindu woman will spend a long time rubbing and massaging her hair and scalp with oil and herbs before bathing. A lot of effort is then put into combing and plaiting. There are many different styles of plaiting and knotting hair. Grooming each other's hair is an ancient practice and a gesture of friendship and even now ladies visiting a friend's house will sometimes do each other's hair. They relax, gossip and chew **pan** (betel) while doing this."

"So they don't go to a hairdresser?" asked Anna, surprised.

"No. Very few Hindu ladies will go to a hairdresser. I have never been to one, nor has Sikha."

Sikha added, "It is a part of our tradition. The art of grooming is learned and mastered within the family, beginning in childhood. In Britain, unfortunately, a lot of Hindu girls have cut their hair and adopted Western hairstyles."

"Why?" asked Anna. "Don't they like having long hair?"

"Long hair needs looking after. For some it is too much of a chore. So they follow the trend and go for the most convenient style – easy to wash, easy to dry and so on," Sikha replied.

Mrs Datta said, "In some parts of India, particularly in the South, girls like to wear flowers in their hair. Some make garlands which are woven in with their plaits, while others simply pin the flowers in the knot at the nape of their neck. The glitter of their saris, the dazzle and jingle of their ornaments and the sweet-smelling flowers in their hair create an atmosphere which can be experienced only in India, but you would not be too disappointed if you went to a Hindu wedding ceremony in Britain where the girls were wearing traditional dress."

"Just one more thing: if it is not too personal, please could you tell me about the keys tied to your sari?"

"I told you, Mummy. They do look a bit odd," laughed Sikha.

Mrs Datta explained, "The housewife enjoys a position of authority in a traditional Hindu household. She manages the day-to-day administration and the keys are for the locks to all her cupboards and boxes. As soon as she enters her husband's household after her marriage, he hands over the keys to her with the utmost trust. Later, as she gains more experience in the affairs of the family and the property, and her parents-in-law become

Hindu women in kameez and close-fitting fitting trousers

older and prefer to spend more time in prayer and worship, they too hand over their keys to their daughter-in-law. She is called 'Ma' or 'Mother' by all her domestic staff. Besides, with more responsibility and more boxes and chests to look after, the number of keys increases and the bunch gets bigger and heavier. The sari has no pockets, you see, so we tie the keys to a corner of the sari and let them hang over the shoulder. The bunch of keys has become a part of our costume, because it holds the sari in place, I suppose. When passed over the shoulder it keeps the hair tidy as well as the sari."

73

8
Ganesh Chaturthi

One day, while visiting an Indian sweetshop in Willesden, Anna was fascinated by a beautiful statue of the same elephant-headed god she had seen at Sikha's house. The god was placed high on the wall in a very attractive chariot-shaped wooden holder. Near the deity a small lamp was burning and an incense-stick smouldered. There were fresh flowers and in front of the statue, a little dish of sweets. The shop, too, had a festive look about it. There were colourful mobiles hanging from the ceiling and paper-chains and tinsel decorated the counter and the walls.

The shopkeeper's wife, Mrs Gupta, noticed Anna and asked, "Do you like our god?"

"Yes, I do," she replied. "Is it a special occasion today? Your shop looks very attractive. It seems that your god is being worshipped."

Mrs Gupta was pleased by Anna's genuine interest and by her politeness. She told her: "Today is **Ganesh Chaturthi**, Lord Ganesha's birthday. Ganesha is the remover of obstacles and a god of wisdom and prosperity. We worship him today so that he may bless this house and bring us good luck. Children like him very much and believe that by worshipping him they will be blessed with wisdom."

"Does Chaturthi mean 'birthday'?" asked Anna.

"No, it means 'fourth day'. Today is the fourth day of Bhadra, the fifth month of our Hindu calendar," said Mrs Gupta.

"Why does Ganesha have an elephant's head?"

"Well, there is a story which tells us that Lord Shiva's wife, Parvati, did not like being interrupted by visitors when she took her bath. So she asked her son to stand guard outside while she washed herself. When Lord Shiva returned he, too, was duly stopped at the gate by his son. Shiva was so outraged that he immediately cut off the boy's head.

74

Statue of Ganesha in Kurda Road, Puri

"When Parvati saw what had happened she cried bitterly and begged Shiva to bring her son back to life. Shiva had realized the rashness of his action. He hurriedly left Parvati, promising to replace the boy's head with the head of the first creature he came across. That creature happened to be an elephant. Lord Shiva cut off its head and fixed it on his son's body. The boy came back to life at once, but Parvati was none too pleased to see him in his present form. So, to please Parvati, Lord Shiva made his son Lord of the Multitude and called him Ganesha, or Ganapati (gana means 'multitude', eesha means 'lord' and pati means 'leader')."

"That was a very interesting story. Thank you," said Anna. "I have taken up a lot of your time. I only came to buy some **ladoo**."

"Here you are," said Mrs Gupta, handing Anna a bag of the sweets, "take some ladoo, but today you are our guest, so please have them as my gift on the occasion of Ganesh Chaturthi. And take some of these. They are savoury. We call them 'chhaura' or 'chanachoor'. You'll like them."

Then she added, "I never imagined that one day I would be telling the story of the Lord to a European girl on this auspicious day! You are very special to me, my child."

Anna was so thrilled by this experience that she sang almost all the way home. She rang up Sikha and asked, "Do you know it's Ganesh Chaturthi today?"

"Yes, but how did *you* know?" answered Sikha, astonished.

"I just do. Can you come over this afternoon?" asked Anna.

"I suppose I could. Why?"

"I just thought that you might like to try some delicious ladoo and chhaura to celebrate Ganesh Chaturthi. Perhaps you'd like to know why Ganesha has an elephant's head, too. But how can I tell you if you don't come over?" Anna teased her.

"Pardon? Try some what?" Sikha was all agog, but all she got from Anna was: "Bye. See you soon!"

9
Food

"Let me show you how to make a very simple non-vegetarian dish," said Mr Datta. "But first you must learn to identify all the ingredients that are going to be used."

Anna looked at the display on the kitchen table and said, "These are the easy ones: onions, garlic, minced meat, tomatoes, peas and vegetable oil."

"That's right," replied Mr Datta. "And you can get them at any supermarket, but you may have to go to an Asian grocer to get the others." He pointed them out: "Root ginger, coriander leaves, green chillies, chilli powder, powdered turmeric, garam masala and ghee (clarified butter)."

"I have been told that chillies are very hot, and here you have both the fresh green ones and the powdered red chillies. Are we going to make a very hot dish?" Anna enquired anxiously.

Mr Datta was quite amused by her concern, but he reassured her, saying, "No, not unless you like very hot food. You see, many people seem to think that all Indian food is very hot. This is not true at all. They also think that all Indian seasonings are more or less the same. That is why they buy a tin of so-called curry powder and keep it in the larder. From time to time they add a spoonful or two to a meat or vegetable stew and serve it as a curry. Nothing is more disastrous than using curry powder!"

"Why? What is in curry powder, and why do people use it?"

"To be quite honest with you, I don't know," said Mr Datta, "but I think that whoever invented it must have realized that there are certain herbs and spices which are essential to Indian cooking, such as turmeric, ginger, cumin, coriander and chilli. To these they added fenugreek, mustard, cloves and a few others. To make a curry powder, spices like these were dried, ground and mixed up in varying proportions to suit Western tastes.

"However, each of these ingredients has its own individual colour, flavour and taste. The spices do not often blend well together, but in curry powder they are forced together, producing a mixture that can only be described as 'strangely piquant'. Any connoisseur of Indian cooking, and especially the housewife, may even find it offensive!

"Amazingly, this concoction appealed to many people, particularly those who fancied Indian food but did not want to go to too much trouble. There were also those who weren't fussy about the 'authenticity' of the food itself but just wanted something spicy and hot, something different from the usual roasted, boiled, fried or stewed European food. Curry powder continues to be produced in large quantities, but the spices and herbs used are not always of the best quality. Besides, left over a long period of time their flavour deteriorates. You can well imagine what happens when curry powder is added to your cooking!"

"It must make it taste awful," agreed Anna.

"Not exactly awful, but certainly not right," Mr Datta replied. "You see, we have a whole variety of spices, herbs and aromatics. They all have their own distinct qualities. Some will blend nicely together and bring out the very best in a certain dish while others may ruin it completely. With curry powder all preparations taste the same. Cooking is an art. Only a person with a thorough knowledge of spices will be able to create authentic Indian cuisine. Now you can try an Indian dish for yourself.

"We have here 500 grams of minced lamb, one large onion, two cloves of garlic and a piece of fresh root ginger about 2 centimetres long. Chop the onion, but not too finely. Crush the garlic and the ginger. Don't forget to peel the ginger first! My goodness! Your eyes are watering already!"

"It's the onions!" said Anna apologetically.

"Never mind. You'll soon get used to it," Mr Datta encouraged her. "Now put two tablespoons of water in that saucepan, and add the mince, onions, garlic and ginger. Cook the mixture for twenty minutes over a medium heat. Keep stirring, so that it doesn't stick to the pan."

While they waited, Mr Datta chopped the tomatoes and then showed Anna how to prepare the herbs and spices used in Indian cookery.

"Let's see," he said. "Yes, that looks all right. The meat looks dry and well cooked. Take it off the heat and put it aside. Now put a tablespoon of vegetable oil in the saucepan and warm it. Add the two finely chopped tomatoes. You could use half a teaspoon of tomato purée instead, by the way."

"What about the spices?"

"Yes, we will put some in now, but only two – just under half a teaspoon of turmeric and one teaspoon of garam masala. At this stage you also decide how hot you want the dish to be. For this amount of meat you could use just half a teaspoon of chilli powder or one fresh green chilli, to make it mildly hot. Add a teaspoon of salt and cook for about two minutes.

"Now add a cupful of peas, fresh or frozen but never tinned peas. When the peas have cooked for another five minutes, add the mince and cook for a further ten minutes."

"Is it ready now?" asked Anna about fifteen minutes later.

"No, not quite," replied Mr Datta. "You haven't prepared the fresh coriander leaves. Chop some finely. When we have transferred the meat into a serving-dish, we'll garnish it with chopped coriander. And there's your keema matar."

"Pardon?"

Mr Datta laughed. "Keema means 'minced meat' and matar means 'peas'. It is a North Indian preparation. You may cook it using green pepper instead of peas," he said. "Now you must write down the recipe in your own words. You have to be bold and inventive and realize that while you are still learning, a slight variation here and there will not make a lot of difference to the taste. But you must use the correct spices."

"It wasn't as difficult to cook as I'd expected," said Anna, "but would you call it a true Hindu preparation?"

"I'm not sure what you mean," answered Mr Datta. "Are you worried because it contains meat?" Anna nodded. "Well, not all Hindus are vegetarians. We are not, as you can see. Also, the way food is prepared varies from one part of the country to another. Thus a North Indian Hindu from Punjab or Uttar Pradesh will prepare his food in a very different way from his South Indian counterpart from Madras or Kerala."

"Most of my friends believe that all Hindus are vegetarians," said Anna.

"That is probably because they think of Hindus as worshippers

79

of gods and goddesses, making vegetarian offerings of fruit, sweets, rice and flowers during a puja. Most Hindus are not vegetarians, in fact," said Mr Datta.

"How did Indians first become vegetarians?"

"It is difficult to say. It certainly had nothing to do with the Vedic age. There are ample examples in the Vedic stories to suggest that in the past all Hindus – including the sages – were meat-eaters. There are even references to the eating of cow flesh!

"It was probably with the growth of Jainism that people stopped eating meat. Jains were influenced by the principle of ahimsa, 'non-violence', and refrained from taking life of any kind. Also, the followers of Vishnu, called 'Vaishnavs', began to worship Krishna, who is an incarnation of Vishnu, in the form of a cowherd. Thus the cow became a holy animal and began to be respected as 'the mother' and the giver of milk. That is why Hindus considered it a great sin to consume the flesh of the cow. Mahatma Gandhi was committed to vegetarianism and many of those who were converted to his philosophy naturally became vegetarians.

Radha offering curds to Krishna

80

"I shall tell you more as we go along, but right now, would you like to try a simple vegetarian preparation – or have you learned enough for one day?"

Anna was far too absorbed to stop yet. "Yes please," she said eagerly, "I would love to try another dish."

"That's good. Now look at this vegetable," said Mr Datta. "It has several names. Some call it 'okra', others 'bhindi'. In Bengali, we call it 'dhandos'. But it has an English name too."

"Does it?"

"Yes. Let me show you," said Mr Datta. He picked up a piece of brown paper and cut out a piece shaped like the palm of a hand. Then he selected five bhindis from the packet and placed them carefully round it, and asked, "Well, what does it look like?"

"It's a hand, and the bhindis are the fingers!"

"Whose fingers?" Mr Datta asked.

"I don't know. A lady's, I suppose, since men don't have such narrow fingers."

"Precisely!" cried Mr Datta triumphantly. "That's exactly what they are called: lady's fingers! The name is thought to have been invented in the days of the British Empire by an Englishman who wanted his Indian servant to get this vegetable from the market. He did not know its name, and the servant did not understand him when he tried to describe it. So, out of sheer frustration, the gentleman took his wife's hand and showed him the long, slender fingers of her hand with their manicured nails. He asked the servant to bring back the green vegetables that looked like the lady's fingers. The servant understood him at once and said, 'Ah! You mean "bhindi", Sir?' And that's how the vegetable came to be known as 'lady's fingers'."

"How fascinating!" Anna chuckled. "You have stories for everything!"

"Well, it's all about knowing different peoples and their ways, isn't it? Now let us get on with the cooking," said Mr Datta briskly. "You know some of the spices already. I shall introduce you to a few more. This is cumin and these are black mustard seds. We need only one teaspoonful of each and we shall use them whole. Now the ground spices: half a teaspoon each of turmeric and coriander. We must also crush together three cloves of garlic, one small piece of root ginger and one green chilli. The recipe says two green chillies and half a teaspoon of red-chilli

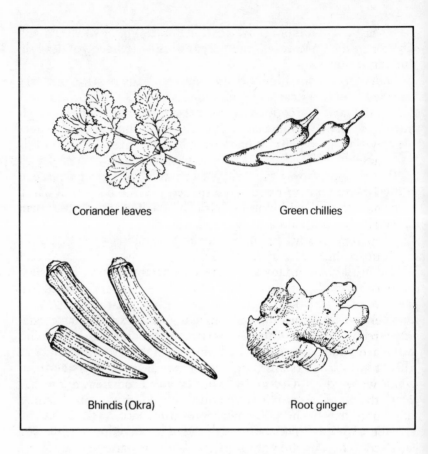

Coriander leaves

Green chillies

Bhindis (Okra)

Root ginger

powder, but you may find that quite hot. You'll have to decide now."

Anna thought for a moment and said, "Just one green chilli, please."

"Good! We'll take this medium-sized one," said Mr Datta. "Once all the spices are ready, the cooking process is very simple. It will be ready in just over fifteen minutes. First, peel, wash and dice three potatoes. Also wash 200 grams of lady's fingers and cut them into small pieces. Next, take four tablespoons of vegetable oil. Heat it in a saucepan. Now add the cumin and the mustard seeds. They will pop, but don't panic – it stops as soon as you put in the potatoes. Keep stirring. Now turn the heat to medium and put the lid on."

"What about the lady's fingers?" Anna asked.

"When the potatoes have cooked for ten minutes, you add the bhindis, but do not cover the pan. Continue stirring until they are soft. At this stage, add all the other spices, both powdered and crushed. Add one teaspoon of salt and one of sugar and stir well. When the food has cooked for another six minutes or so, it will be ready to serve. You may, if you like, sprinkle some chopped parsley on top when you have transferred it into a serving-dish. We shall not bother about the parsley today, as we haven't got any."

"It is so simple." Anna looked surprised.

"That's what I said," smiled Mr Datta. "This is a Gujarati dish. It is called 'bhindi-aloo' (aloo means 'potato'). In Bengal it would be prepared slightly differently, but both versions are delicious!"

Just then Mrs Datta, Sikha and Goutam arrived. They had been to the Bengali school to carry out their Sunday duties.

"How are you getting on with your cookery lesson?" asked Mrs Datta.

"Very well, thank you," replied Anna excitedly. "I have prepared two dishes – one vegetarian and one non-vegetarian."

"Have you? I can smell the bhindis," Mrs Datta said with an expert air. "It looks as though you have been working very hard while we were out. Go and join your friends and have a rest. I shall serve the food in about half an hour."

Goutam and Sikha were delighted by Anna's efforts.

"We are sorry that we could not keep you company while you were cooking, but did you enjoy it?" Goutam enquired.

"I enjoyed it very much, thank you. Mr Datta is a very good teacher."

"Yes, he is," Sikha agreed. "He is an excellent cook, and because his interest in cooking developed quite recently, since he came to Britain, he can explain things from his own experience and in a simple way. He loves to experiment with different ideas, new recipes. With Mummy, however, it is different. She learned to cook when she was only about eight or nine, from her mother and grandmother. Her knowledge of spices and herbs and all the other ingredients is so sound and her ideas of mixing them so accurate that she can almost taste the dish while she is still planning it. The range of dishes she can cook is far more extensive than Daddy's, too."

"I envy you both," said Anna, "having two such great cooks in the family!"

"Both Sikha and I can cook, but we are lucky to have learned the art from our own parents," Goutam replied.

The food was now ready. Anna was surprised by the number of dishes on the table. There were the two she had cooked, but there were four more, besides the plate of rice and the mixed salad! She couldn't work out how so many items had been prepared in half an hour! Mrs Datta explained that she had cooked them the night before. They only needed to be warmed up.

As they sat down at the table Mr Datta said, "Your two preparations are the main dishes this afternoon, Anna. The others are just supplementary ones."

"That makes me quite nervous!"

"Have confidence, my dear," Mr Datta reassured her. "Besides, if anything goes wrong, I'll have to share the blame with you, since I am your teacher. Let me, however, go back to your question about Hindu food. At the moment, there are eight items in front of us. Only the keema matar and the prawn patoori are non-vegetarian dishes. The dal, the bhindi aloo, the aubergine and onion pakora and the matar paneer are vegetarian dishes. They are all delicious and perfectly acceptable to non-vegetarian Hindus like us.

"It is only beef that is generally unacceptable to the Hindus, in spite of what I said about the Vedic age. Most Hindus do not prepare beef or pork in their kitchens. As you know, the cow is considered sacred by the Hindus. The pig, on the other hand, is regarded as unclean, because it forages in gutters and other dirty places. Neither the minced meat nor the prawns we are eating today would be acceptable to vegetarians – strict vegetarians won't even touch eggs."

Sikha interrupted her father, saying, "An egg has life too!"

"Yes, that is why some vegetarians will not eat eggs, while others argue that although an egg has life, that life has not yet developed consciousness. Even trees and plants have life! But, leaving aside the religious or moral aspects of food, the Hindus believe that in order to lead a normal, healthy life one must eat only natural food, free from preservatives. The right combination of foods will provide the protein, fat, carbohydrates and vitamins that a normal person needs. Anything eaten in excess

84

is either wasted or is harmful. Those who eat thoughtlessly put on a lot of weight and suffer from indigestion, heart trouble, high blood pressure and so on."

"How do you find out which foods have the properties you're looking for?" Goutam asked.

"The ancient Hindus spent a lot of time studying those things and in the Puranic stories there are many references to food," answered Mr Datta. "Take lemon and honey, for instance. We all know that they have both curative and preventive qualities and are used for coughs and colds."

"But that is like medicine," Anna remarked.

"Exactly!" replied Mr Datta. "Our predecessors believed that their food was their medicine, and their medicine their food. In other words, if you take the right sort of food in the right quantity it will protect your body against disease.

"Now then, let us separate the vegetables, the meat and the spices and see what we are eating today!"

"Oh, Daddy! Do you have to do that?" Sikha complained, but Anna was most enthusiastic.

"Why not?" she said. "It'll be fun!"

Mrs Datta, who had been quietly serving everyone, gave her husband a look and said, "I know what Sikha means. And before you start analysing your food I would like to say to Anna that both her preparations are absolutely delicious! You are all so busy talking that you probably haven't even noticed!"

"Sorry, Anna," they all murmured, shame-faced.

"You must come every Sunday," added Goutam. "If this is what you can produce on your very first day, can you imagine what will happen when you've had lots of practice?"

They all laughed.

"All right, then," said Mr Datta, "let's examine just one dish, the bhindi-aloo. First, the vegetables: lady's fingers and potatoes. Then the green spices: garlic, ginger and green chillies. Finally, the dried spices: mustard, turmeric, cumin and coriander.

"*Lady's fingers:* these strengthen muscles – they are full of vitamins – they purify the blood and reduce heartburn.

"*Potatoes:* these create albumen and also reduce the impurities in blood.

"*Green chillis* prevent indigestion and diarrhoea and increase body heat.

85

"*Green ginger* cures arthritis and bile disorders and is good for coughs.

"*Garlic:* this is full of vitamins, prevents flatulence and assists the function of the bowels.

"*Mustard* also prevents flatulence and is a preventive against leprosy.

"*Turmeric* improves the complexion and has very high healing properties.

"*Cumin* helps digestion.

"Finally, *coriander:* this prevents infestation by thread-worms."

"How did you remember all that?" Anna asked. She was obviously very impressed.

Mr Datta said, "When I was a little boy an old Brahmin used to visit us in the village. I used to listen to him with great interest when he explained these things to my mother. Not only that – he used to treat cuts and bites and fever simply with certain herbs and food. And all for a cup of tea and a bowl of moa-mudi (sweetened puffed rice)! He was so knowledgeable that we used to call him Uncle Encyclopaedia!"

A woman sits by the tulsi plant while the family priest prepares for the puja. The children wait for their share of the prasaad of moa-mudi.

Anna burst out laughing, but apologized at once: "Sorry, I couldn't help it. What a funny name!"

"I don't mind," said Mr Datta. He was laughing too. "The trouble is that the beneficial properties of herbs and food are lost during cooking," he continued, "especially if they are fried. I hope you will now appreciate why such great care is necessary in cooking. In the past, devout Hindus used to prefer a diet of plain, unspiced food consisting of boiled and mashed vegetables and pulses supplemented with milk, nuts and fruit. They called this type of food 'satwik', or 'pure and healthy'. They despised food that was overcooked and enriched or garnished with heavy spices and aromatics. Such food was called 'rajasik', implying that it was fit only for those who indulged in the pleasures of life. The most inferior form of food was called 'tamasik'. This was usually stale and devoid of all nutritional value, and its only purpose was to excite the palate of people with a weakness for rich food."

"I wonder what those devout Hindus would think of our menu today," remarked Anna.

"Well, the non-vegetarian dishes would be rejected, for a start, but I'm afraid that the other items would also come under attack for containing rajasik elements, because of the way they have been spiced. However," continued Mr Datta, "we are not following the exact footsteps of our forefathers, nor are we looking into the religious basis of everything we eat. We can use any spices we like, but in moderation."

Eating in traditional style

Mrs Datta had left the table a few minutes earlier. Now she returned with a small piece of brightly coloured wool carpet about sixty centimetres square and asked Anna if she could guess what it was used for. Anna took it from her and examined it. It was light and beautifully designed. The pink, red and blue woollen patterns in the shape of lotus petals were tufted and skilfully cropped.

"What a lovely carpet! Is it used as a floor mat, to sit on?" she guessed.

"You are absolutely right!" said Mrs Datta. "In well-to-do Hindu homes mats like this are used on special occasions. They are placed on the floor for honoured guests to sit on while they eat. They are also offered to a new bride or bridegroom, or to the child at the Anna Prashan ceremony. This one was made about sixty years ago by my mother-in-law, when she was a young house-wife."

"Sixty years!" Anna exclaimed. "But it looks so fresh!"

"It does! It is not only beautiful, but a part of our tradition. You see, in order to enjoy an Indian meal you should create the right atmosphere. Sitting at a table like this, using dinner-plates and eating Indian food with knives and forks, is not at all traditional. I am sure you know that already."

"Yes, I do, but to be quite honest, I didn't think that you had your meals any other way," Anna replied, hoping she wasn't being tactless.

The Dattas had to admit this was true. Mrs Datta added, "Let me tell you a bit about our customs. Then you will see why it is difficult to practise them over here, although not absolutely impossible.

"If you think back to the Anna Prashan ceremony you attended with us you will understand most of the things I say. Remember the mat on which the little boy sat, and the large plate with the rice and lots of other dishes, a pinch of salt and a piece of lemon. The plate was surrounded by several small- to medium-sized bowls for a whole variety of dishes, most of which contained sauce or gravy. Finally, there was a beaker for drinking-water."

"I can remember all those things very clearly, although at the time I was quite overwhelmed by the whole atmosphere," said Anna. "After all, it was my very first experience of a Hindu ceremony!"

"Well, the basic arrangements remain the same, but the details vary, for several reasons," went on Mrs Datta. "For example, the way the food is prepared and served differs according to people's eating habits, and the utensils used will range from silverware – for the extremely well-to-do – to the banana leaves and saal leaves used for plates and bowls in the villages."

"Plates and bowls made from leaves!" echoed Anna in disbelief.

"Yes, and they are lovely, too! The leaves of the banana tree are quite large and strong. You can easily cut out four to six mats from one leaf. You cut a whole leaf from the plant with a sharp knife, split it into two halves by cutting along its spine, and cut the sections you want from each half. Then you wash them and wipe them and use them as plates. It is so easy!"

"How fascinating! And the bowls?" asked Anna.

88

"They're almost as easy to make. You take a small, squarish piece of leaf, pinch the edges together and fold them over. You secure each fold by pushing a thin twig, like a toothpick, through it. By repeating this at three or four corners you make a bowl. The leaves of the saal tree are best for bowls but the plantain leaves are better for eating-mats, used instead of plates.

"Disposable plates and bowls made from leaves are very popular, especially at Hindu ceremonies where hundreds of people sit down to eat together. Disposable clay bowls and beakers for drinking-water are also used on these occasions. The clay pots and the eating-mats are bought at village markets or at grocer's shops.

"In England it is usual to have only one plate for each course. For example, you help yourself from the serving-dishes to meat, potatoes and vegetables and put them all on one plate. We, on the other hand, serve each person at the beginning of the meal and keep all the items separate. Everyone has a main plate surrounded by several small bowls, each containing a different item.

"Further helpings are served by whoever is attending the diners, usually the mother, a daughter, a daughter-in-law or all three. It gives them a lot of pleasure to see that their cooking is being appreciated. They usually sit nearby with a palm-leaf, fanning the plate and, occasionally, the diner. They drive away the ever-pestering flies and serve their husbands, children and guests with

Men using leaf-plates and clay beakers in Orissa

loving care, often coaxing them to 'a little bit of this and some more of that'."

"You eat with your fingers, don't you?" asked Anna.

"Yes, that is correct," confirmed Mrs Datta. "If you sit cross-legged on the floor and the food is placed in front of you, you have to lean over to reach it. It would be most inconvenient to use any cutlery in this position. Besides, our preparations often contain gravy and are usually scooped up with a piece of chapati. With rice dishes, however, a small amount of the meat or vegetables is mixed with the rice and eaten with the fingers.

"We always wash our hands and rinse our mouths before and after every meal. Eating with your fingers is a skill and is acquired from childhood. If you are good at it you dip only your fingertips in the food, keeping the rest of your hand clean and dry. Some people are less tidy in their habits."

"Do you have the equivalent of desserts?"

"At the end of the main course we serve a chutney made from mangoes, pawpaws, tomatoes and dates," said Mrs Datta. "Afterwards you might have a rice pudding called 'payesh', or thickened milk called 'kheer' mixed with mango pulp, orange-segments, etc., or sweetened yoghurt. Finally, there is a whole range of sweetmeats to choose from. The most popular is the famous rasogolla, which literally means 'sweet-balls in syrup'."

"Oh yes! They are so delicious that I always forget that I shouldn't have more than one or two," said Anna.

Mrs Datta smiled and said, "I am glad you reminded me. We have some to eat now." She asked Goutam to fetch them and continued: "The Bengalis are by far the best sweetmeat-makers in the country. It is their speciality. There are so many varieties that I cannot remember even a fraction of them. Even their names are mouth-watering! For example: sandesh, which means 'news', and ledikeni which, like 'lady's fingers', was probably coined during the days of the Raj, meaning 'Lady Kenny's favourite'. There are two others, called 'Mohan Bhog' and 'Gopal Bhog'. Both these names mean 'Lord Krishna's favourite prasaad'. And what about pran hara, which means 'the one that steals your heart'?"

"They are delightful names! What a pity no one makes them over here," sighed Sikha.

"Only the names of some of the English roses would match their style," agreed Mr Datta. "All those sweets are truly delicious!

However sumptuous an Indian meal may be," he continued, "it is always washed down with plain water, nothing else. You have learned about the properties of various ingredients of our food. According to Uncle Encyclopaedia, water is light, cool, refreshing, it quenches thirst and reduces fatigue. It also dilutes the strength of so many spices in the food, therefore it helps digestion.

"At the end of a meal it is customary to offer betels and aromatics to chew. They neutralize the taste of the food in the mouth and prevent bad breath."

"What are betels?" Anna asked.

"The betel is a delicate tropical creeper with juicy leaves. On its own the pan (betel leaf) tastes sharp and bitter, but it has great medicinal qualities. There is a particular type of nut called 'supari', or areca-nut, which is used only with betel. Hence it is also called the 'betel-nut'. Betel leaves are stuffed with a pinch of dessicated betel-nut, some roasted coriander, fennel seed, cardamom, cloves and cinnamon, smeared with lime and a special paste called 'khayer', and chewed after a meal. Those who use tobacco also put a pinch of roasted coriander seeds treated with the essence of tobacco in their betel leaf. Smokers usually collect in small groups and wander off to light a cigarette or a bidi. Bidis are mini-cigars made by rolling shredded tobacco in a leaf of a plant. Smoking in the presence of the elders is generally frowned upon. In the villages you sometimes see men smoking a hubble-bubble. Women do not smoke at all.

"That concludes a Hindu meal, or even an Indian meal!"

10
Dussera

As Mr Datta walked through the door Sikha literally pounced on him and snatched the carrier-bag from his hand. Inside there were three beautiful saris.

"Thanks, Daddy! They're lovely! I'll take this one!" She was bubbling with excitement.

"But that one is for your mother!" he protested.

"Oh please, Dad – please, Mum – may I? *Please?*"

There are very few parents who would not give in to a beloved daughter's demands, especially at this time of the year. It was **Dussera**, also known as **Durga Puja** or **Navaratri** (Nine Nights).

Mrs Datta did not mind which of the other two saris she had. They were both very nice.

"What about the third one? Who is going to wear it?" Sikha wanted to know.

Mrs Datta said, "I hope you haven't forgotten your friend at this festival season!"

"Anna – of course!" Sikha shrieked with delight. "She'll look absolutely lovely!"

Goutam and Mr Datta would be wearing suits, although in India they would have worn a dhoti and a kurta.

After dinner, Mrs Datta made two choli blouses, one for Anna and the other for Sikha. She is an expert dressmaker, but it still took her almost three hours to cut and stitch them.

The following day Goutam, Sikha and Anna went straight to the Dattas' after school. Anna had no idea of what was in store. Mrs Datta arrived shortly afterwards. They all had to have a wash and tidy their hair in preparation for the big occasion. As Anna came out of the bathroom, Mrs Datta called her into her bedroom.

"You must change into this, Anna," she said, producing the sari.

"My goodness! Is that for me?" Anna couldn't believe her eyes.

"Yes, it's our Durga Puja present for you."

"Thank you so much. It is beautiful! But I don't think I can put it on properly by myself," stammered Anna, blushing.

Mrs Datta and Sikha helped her with the sari. The new outfit suited Anna very well, and as soon as he arrived home, Mr Datta admired her new image, saying, "Well, well! And who is this lovely girl?"

They all set out for the old town hall in Hampstead.

"Remember this place?" Goutam asked Anna. "I told you about our big Durga Puja celebrations on our way to the Anna Prashan ceremony."

Goutam was quite right about it being a popular festival – there were cars parked all along Haverstock Hill and in every side-street, hundreds of them! As the Dattas walked through the main door they saw an enormous crowd of men, women and children, all in their best clothes, hair-styles and jewellery – a unique combination of colour, glitter, music and noise! There were rows and rows of chairs in the main hall, and on the dais stood the beautiful images of the deities. There was the goddess Durga on her mount, a ferocious lion, slaying the demon Mahishasura. On her right were Lakshmi and Ganesha, and on her left Saraswati

Pith-work statues of Durga slaying the buffalo demon Mahishasura from her mount, the lion (Wembley, Middlesex)

93

and Kartik. The area in front of the dais was decorated with alpana patterns and objects including brass and copper utensils, fruit and flowers. The priest was seated in front of the goddess chanting hymns and prayers.

Anna was introduced to so many of the Dattas' friends that she virtually lost count of them. They all admired her beautiful sari and were impressed by her courteous manner and her interest in the puja.

Anna was invited back to the Dattas' house the following evening to see how they observed the Durga Puja fast and offered flowers to the goddess. This was **Mahastami**, the eighth day of the puja. On this day the celebrations reach their climax. Durga's tremendous power is felt by all the devotees who seek the goddess's forgiveness for their sins and weaknesses and the goddess calms their emotion with her blessings.

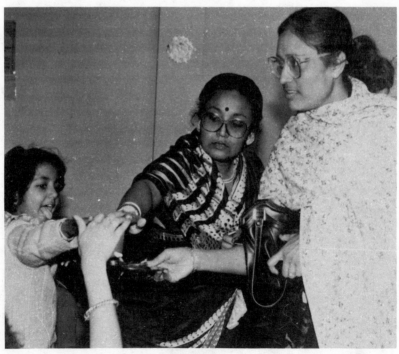

Devotees holding their hands over the burning lamp at the end of Durga Puja

94

Anna learned how the evil forces represented by Mahishasura were overcome when Durga emerged from the combined powers of all the gods in heaven to slay the demon. In each of her ten arms she holds either a weapon or an object symbolizing peace and friendship. She has three eyes – one in the middle of her forehead – representing duty, knowledge and happiness.

Anna, Sikha and Goutam experienced a different kind of Durga Puja celebration on the ninth day of the festival.

Sumitra was no longer the shy girl she had been when she joined Heathurst School a few months ago. Sikha and Anna were now two of her closest friends. She had described to them how Durga Puja is celebrated by the Gujarati-speaking community and invited them to join her at the Harrow Leisure Centre, where the huge hall had been hired for this great occasion.

Anna and Sikha arrived at the hall accompanied by Goutam. Sumitra was waiting for them with her brother and sister. Her parents and her uncle's family were to join them later. The girls were wearing beautiful jewellery and some of them had painted the palms of their hands; all the men, women and children were in their best clothes. The hall was packed to capacity. An attractive dais had been erected and on it stood a large and very beautiful picture of the goddess Durga. Several oil-lamps surrounded the goddess, and incense was burning. A group of people were singing devotional songs in praise of the Holy Mother.

Sumitra explained to her guests that the festival of Navaratri begins on the first night of Aswin, the sixth month of the Hindu calendar, and ends on the ninth night. On each of the nine nights one of the goddess's battling forms is worshipped. (She assumed a different form to destroy each of the several immensely powerful demons she encountered.)

Several women came out to perform the arati by lighting lamps and going round the shrine singing hymns. When it was over, people began to take their places to dance round the dais. They adjusted their steps to the beating of the drum and the clapping of hands. Anna, Sikha and Goutam joined in. They found it difficult at first but improved as they went on. Suddenly the music stopped. Someone called out instructions to clear the floor for the stick-dancers. They were a group of very skilful dancers in colourful costumes, holding multi-coloured sticks in their hands. Striking

The Stick Dance (Hindu Centre, London)

their partners' sticks, the dancers formed graceful and intricate patterns to the sound of the beautiful music that played in the background.

The festival ended with a final devotional song in praise of Mother Durga and people began to leave the hall. Everyone was given a small bag of prasaad containing coconut, sweets, a piece of apple and some nuts. It was a very enjoyable evening!

The next day, they all returned to Hampstead for **Vijaya Dashami**, the tenth and last day of the puja. On this day there is a farewell celebration – called 'Visharjan' – for the goddess. After the Visharjan people embrace each other and exchange greetings. In Bengali this gesture is called 'kola-kuli'. The younger ones go round and touch their elders' feet as a mark of respect. This is called 'pranaam'. Traditionally, it is acknowledged by offering sweetmeats. The celebration is held in honour of the goddess's vijaya (victory). It ends with a performance of song and dance by local artistes.

Anna felt she understood the spirit of the festival. Everyone's thoughts were focused on the theme of Durga Puja. Even the

Kola-kuli embrance on the final day of the festival (Wembley, Middlesex)

smallest children knew what was going on and why they were there. Many of them became cross and tearful when their parents wanted to go home. For Anna it was a marvellous occasion, even though Mr Datta kept saying that somehow it lacked the atmosphere of celebrations held in India!

11
An Engagement Ceremony

The drawling note of **shanai** music greeted Anna when she arrived at the Dattas'.

"What's going on?" she asked her friend.

"I have good news for you!" Sikha said excitedly. "You've met our friend Anil, haven't you? Well, he's getting engaged next week, so you will have an opportunity to see a Hindu wedding – a Bengali wedding, in fact! Right now Daddy is selecting some music which will be played at the wedding."

"Really? When will it be? Who is the lucky girl?" Anna asked.

"Probably next February or March. The engagement ceremony will take place in Barnet, and you know the girl! It's Gouri – you remember, the one at the Durga Puja celebrations with that beautiful sari," Sikha prompted her friend.

The music stopped. Mr Datta came out to say hello.

"You have heard the news, of course, Anna. I am absolutely delighted. How time passes!" he said, shaking his head. "When his parents left for India, Anil stayed on to finish his O-levels and now he has got his Ph.D. and is about to get married! His father and I come from the same neighbourhood in India. I have known Anil since he was a child. We are very proud of him!"

"Yes, I thought he seemed very nice," agreed Anna. "What about Gouri?"

"Ah – Gouri! I met her father by chance, at the National Film Theatre. We chatted over coffee and became friends. He was then, as he is now, a consultant engineer and Gouri was trying to get into medical school. They are a very cultured family. Gouri has finished her degree course now. Besides, she is twenty-four, an age that makes parents think about their daughter's future. When I mentioned Anil to them, they simply jumped at the idea!"

"I hope that Anil and Gouri also jumped at the idea," Anna commented drily.

Mr Datta was surprised by Anna's remark. There was a sceptical note in her voice. It suddenly dawned on him that Sikha and Anna were two girls growing up in modern Britain. They were very mature in outlook and were worried that Gouri and Anil might not agree with their parents' wishes – one or both of them might be unwilling to marry.

"Well, no. Not straight away," he said. "They didn't even know each other at that time. I decided to play the role of **ghatak** – matchmaker. The ghatak plays an important part in Hindu weddings."

Anna relaxed a little. "Please tell me a bit more," she asked Mr Datta.

"A professional ghatak keeps a register of marriageable girls and young men, with details of their family backgrounds, education, health, jobs, etc. When parents contact them, they arrange an introduction, for which they charge a fee. The meeting often takes place at the girl's home.

"On the appointed day, the girl is brought out, looking her best, before a host of strangers. Sweating and trembling, she is asked all sorts of questions, some straightforward, others rather tricky and embarrassing! Once the interviewers are satisfied, marriage negotiations may begin."

"How awful!" cried Anna. "Poor girl – it's as bad as a job interview!"

"No. It is, in fact, far worse," Mr Datta corrected her. "However, let me assure you that things have changed considerably in recent years. Now, although a lot of the marriage proposals are initiated in the traditional manner, the meeting may take place at a party or at a social gathering. Anil and Gouri met at our house. Anil's parents were spending a week with us and we invited Gouri and her parents down from Edinburgh. The two families got to know each other well and we proceeded from there."

Anna looked much happier now. She told Mr Datta, "We have heard so much about marriages arranged by parents against their children's will. I was afraid this might be just such a case. I am sorry."

"Don't apologize, Anna. I understand your concern," he reassured her. "I introduced the two families because Anil's father is like an elder brother to me."

"That's nice," said Anna. "I hope both Anil and Gouri will be very happy."

"We hope so too. Next week you'll have a chance to find out for yourself. And later on perhaps you would like to come to the wedding?"

"Well, you know the answer to that question, Mr Datta. There's no need to tempt me any further," replied Anna, blushing.

On a bitterly cold Sunday morning in November a party of ten people, Anna among them, set off for Barnet. When the cars pulled up outside a fairly large house in Hillside Gardens, they were all given a warm welcome. Gouri's parents came out and greeted Anil's parents. Then everyone was introduced to Anil's uncle and aunt, who had travelled from India specially for the occasion.

In the centre of the lounge lay a gorgeous woollen mat and, nearby, a silver tray containing a handful of dhoob grass and a few grains of paddy (unthreshed rice). An oil-lamp had been lit and a couple of incense sticks were burning. Music played in the background. The atmosphere was festive but calm.

"Where is Gouri?" Anna asked.

"There!" said Sikha.

Gouri stood in the doorway, about to be led to the mat by her mother. She looked elegant in a beautiful silk sari of cream and gold. She was wearing no make-up except for a faint black line drawn along her eyelids to the corner of her eyes, and the maroon dot between her eyebrows. There were a few flowers in her hair. Gracefully, she walked through the door, looking modestly downward, and took her seat on the mat.

"She is very pretty," whispered Anna. Sikha nodded.

Anil's uncle, being the eldest representative of the young man's family, came forward. He took a few blades of grass and a pinch of the paddy grains from the tray and put them on Gouri's head, uttering a few words of blessing. Then he gave her a small box which she received with both hands and acknowledged by touching his feet.

"What's in the box?" asked Anna.

Sikha didn't know, but Goutam explained, "In our custom there is no engagement ring as such, but some jewellery is usually given to the girl as an engagement gift." Anna learned afterwards that Gouri's present was a beautiful gold bracelet set with pearls.

One by one all the elders performed the same ritual to bless Gouri. Anil just stayed in the background and watched, obviously feeling very happy. Now the engagement ceremony was over. By this time people had got to know each other. The atmosphere was more relaxed and far noisier as they all settled down to a hearty late lunch.

On the way back Mr Datta explained to Anna, "What you witnessed today is the prelude to a wedding. Every girl has to be blessed in this way. The young man will be blessed by the bride's parents as he arrives on the day of wedding. Through this ceremony the parents of Gouri and Anil have given their consent to the marriage. It is a solemn promise and an engagement is hardly ever broken. Later on, a day that is both convenient and auspicious will be fixed for the wedding. I think, in this case, it will be some time in February or March."

It was to be a March wedding. The family astrologers in India had examined the horoscopes of Anil and Gouri and declared that they were a compatible pair and that all the signs were favourable to their union. The auspicious hour most favourable for the wedding had been worked out.

"From now on," said Mr Datta, "everything will be organized around the wedding-day. First, we have to hire a hall."

"And that is a great pity," Sikha complained. "In India it would have been celebrated at home. It's much more fun having a wedding at home."

"At home?" Anna was surprised. "Why, don't you go to the temple?" she asked.

"No. According to our custom, the ceremony always takes place at the bride's home," replied Mrs Datta. "Usually it takes place in a courtyard. A colourful canopy called a 'shamiana' is specially erected for this purpose and many rituals are performed."

Mr Datta added, "Yes, many rituals – all according to the Vedic Rules. It is not, however, possible to follow absolutely everything as prescribed in the scriptures. People tend to vary the rites according to their circumstances, but they are always very interesting to watch. I am sure you will enjoy the proceedings."

Anna was most impressed when she received the beautiful, ornate card formally inviting her to the wedding. She learned that the

101

card had been printed in India. Sikha told her that quite a few people, especially Anil's close relatives, were upset because the wedding would be in London and they wouldn't be able to attend. Anil's father was also worried that he might have disappointed a lot of people by his decision.

"Was it out of the question to have the wedding in India?" Anna asked.

"Yes, I'm afraid so. You see, Gouri's parents and all their close relatives are in Britain. Her grandparents are no longer alive and the family has very little contact with India. It wouldn't make sense for them to fly out to India just for the wedding," Sikha explained.

"I see. I hope everyone understands the difficulties," Anna sympathized.

"Oh yes, I'm sure they do. Besides, the prospect of having Gouri as a daughter-in-law compensates for everything! She is such a nice person."

QUESTIONS AND PROJECTS

Chapters 7–11

1 Write a few lines about the Upavita (sacred thread).

2 Explain why vermilion is an important feature of a Hindu woman's make-up.

3 Make a large frieze to show the costumes worn in different parts of India.

4 Design a range of jewellery for the wrist, arm, neck, head and ankles. Base your designs on traditional symbols or motifs from any culture. (The description of Hindu ornaments in Chapter 7 may give you some ideas.)

5 Read some of the many stories about Lord Ganesha and then write one in your own words.

6 Using Mr Datta's recipe, prepare some keema matar or bhindi aloo. (Ask your teacher for help with the shopping and cooking.)

7 The origin of the name "lady's fingers" is an interesting one. Find out whether there are similar stories behind the names of other foods (from any country).

8 Like the Hindus, members of another faith eat only with their right hand. Which faith is it?

9 Following the Bengali style of giving colourful names to food, especially sweets, suggest new names for common cakes and pastries.

10 Anna seemed to dislike the idea of an arranged marriage. Why? Would you be willing to accept a marriage partner chosen by your parents?

11 Write a report about arranged marriages today or in the past, in any part of the world. (For example, in sixteenth- and seventeenth-century Britain the upper classes generally married for money or for political reasons rather than for love.) Use specific examples if you can.

12
Divali

Divali is the Festival of Lights. The word "Divali" comes from the Sanskrit word "deepavali", which means "cluster of lights". Naturally, the festival takes place at night. The Dattas call it **Kali Puja** as they are Bengalis, but for Sumitra, it is Divali. She is Gujarati. Anna is extremely fortunate in having friends in both camps. She can find out how the festival is celebrated in Britain according to the cultural traditions of both the eastern and the western parts of India.

When Anna arrived at their house, Mrs Datta and Sikha were busy cleaning and polishing all the utensils used for their puja. The next job was to remove all the images of the deities from the shrine, clean it carefully, and put the deities back.

Mrs Datta had some rice-flour paste in a small bowl. Anna asked her what she was going to do with it.

"We are going to draw some alpana patterns, but unfortunately, we can only draw them on the doorstep. It cannot be done on carpet."

Goutam's voice could be heard through the back door.

"Has Anna arrived yet?"

"Yes, I have. Hello, Goutam! What on earth are you doing?" asked Anna, looking out into the garden.

Goutam had almost finished arranging a layer of bricks to form a temporary platform at the bottom of the garden.

"We are going to light a small bonfire and some fireworks on this platform," he explained. "The bricks are to stop the lawn being scorched like it was last year. You should have seen Dad – he was like the outraged Lord Shiva! Mind you, I don't blame him. He tends this lawn with great care."

Sikha came out with a box in her hand and said, "Here they are, but only twenty of them!"

Kali on Shiva: a painting from West Bengal

"What are they?" Anna asked. "Your house is full of curios!"

They all laughed, and Sikha told her, "They are not exactly curios, but small earthernware lamps called **pradip** or **diva**. We brought about a hundred from India. They break so easily, though! We lose a few each year and now there are only twenty left."

In every Hindu family the preparations for the festival go on all day. Mrs Datta explained to Anna that throughout India, the main attraction of Divali is illumination, although the customs vary.

"In Bengal the emphasis is on the worship of the goddess Kali," said Mrs Datta. "She is the wife of Lord Shiva and is also another form of Durga – except that Kali is even more ferocious and fearsome than Durga. She wears a garland of severed heads and a skirt of severed arms taken from the numerous demons she has slain and devoured, and her tongue hangs out of her mouth dripping blood. Her thirst for blood is often satisfied through sacrifices. She controls floods, epidemics, storms, earthquakes and evil spirits. Yet she is also the Great Mother, kind and benevolent. Her devotees approach her with caution. They dare not upset her, and try only to please her.

"The day before Kali Puja, in every family fourteen oil-filled lamps are lit in honour of the fourteen generations of their dead ancestors. Another lamp is fixed high up on a pole, lighting up the sky. But the following night, the night of the new moon, row after row of lamps, candles and electric bulbs are lit to decorate buildings, houses and doorways. Everyone, young and old, participates in a wild revelry of fireworks, singing and dancing."

"How wonderful! I can't wait!" said Anna excitedly.

Goutam, being the organizer of the festivities in the Datta household, reminded them, "And don't forget, we are leaving here at eight o'clock to go to Sumitra's place."

That evening Mr Datta took some pictures of Anna and his family celebrating Divali with the fireworks. Then he drove them to Wembley. Sumitra and her brother, her sister and her cousins greeted them as soon as their car pulled up outside the Ealing Road Library.

It was a spectacular sight! The entire length of Ealing Road was crowded with people and festooned with coloured lights just like the Christmas lights in Regent Street! Almost all the shop-fronts were decorated with coloured bulbs and rows of candles shone in

106

the windows. They walked up and down Ealing Road admiring the lights. Then Sumitra's mother invited them to their house to see the puja.

Her father explained: "We worship Lakshmi as well as Lord Ganesha. She is the goddess of wealth and prosperity. The illuminations are in her honour. As you saw when you came in, we have drawn patterns of rice-flour on the doorstep and the path. Because our new working year begins at Divali, we open a new account-book. We also celebrate the festival in honour of Lord Rama's victorious return from Lanka after destroying Ravana, the wicked demon king. On this day Rama was crowned King of Ayoddhya. Children read the famous story of the Ramayana and act out scenes from it. Feasts are held, too. We are all very honoured to have you with us this evening," he added, giving them a large box full of ladoo and other sweet and savoury snacks.

Then it was time to go home, so they all exchanged Divali greetings. As they left Sumitra's house, they stepped into a very noisy world. All along the pavement groups of people were enjoying themselves with lots of fireworks, mostly crackers, fountains and sparklers. Anna would never have imagined such celebrations could go on in the street! In the bright lights of the fireworks hundreds of smiling faces of people from nearly every part of the world could be seen, including some under Metropolitan Police helmets. They were all wishing each other a happy Divali.

Effigy of Ravana, the ten-headed demon king, towering above the houses in Victoria Park, Finchley

107

13
Funeral Rites

Sumitra was so overcome with grief when her grandmother died that she almost made herself ill. She refused all food and for two whole days did not leave her grandmother's empty bedroom. From time to time she would stroke the pillow, pick up her grandmother's Ramayana or play with her beads. Then she would put everything back and straighten the sheets with great care, as she always used to just before Gran went to bed. Her mother tried to persuade her to have something to eat, but in vain.

When Sikha and Anna came to visit their friend, they could see that everyone was worried about her, but her father said, "Leave her alone for a while. No one will ever know what is going through her mind right now, but she should not be disturbed while she mourns her grandmother. I have lost my mother, but I can accept her passing away. She died at a ripe old age.

"It is still too early for Sumitra to accept that, however. Her grandmother was the link between her and the world outside. You see, Mother taught her to eat, talk, play and understand things. Most important of all, she held her hand tightly while the two of them journeyed through the mysterious and captivating world of the Ramayana. No wonder Sumitra holds on to the holy book and the beads in that way! Who is going to be her companion, now that Gran is gone?"

He too broke down, but quickly recovered and said, "I'm sorry, girls. I hope you will understand. I shall tell Sumitra that you called. Thank you both very much."

"Please, but only when you can. There is absolutely no hurry. We understand. Our parents have asked us to express their condolences, too," said Anna.

"That's most kind!"

Both Anna and Sikha were very quiet on the way home. As they closed the front door, Sikha broke the silence.

"I have been thinking of my own grandmother," she said. "She is very old, as you know, and suddenly my mind is filled with memories of our home in India. Rising above everyone and everything comes the recollection of Grandma's loving face and her kind voice. I have become aware of the distance that separates us. In India, I used to be very close to her. Like Sumitra, I also listened to her Ramayana and Mahabharata stories. How she wept when we left to come to Britain! For Sumitra life will never be the same again, you know. The loss of someone so close and so dear will be hard to endure."

Sikha began to cry. Anna had never seen her so upset. She went over to comfort her. Mr Datta, who had heard what his daughter said, came and sat down beside her.

"You see, we take life so much for granted that death, to most of us, seems unexpected and unacceptable," he told her. "Yet, like birth, it is something quite natural. Death is painful for the bereaved because it is a loss which is permanent.

"Sumitra is overwhelmed with grief at this moment because she has just returned from the crematorium where her grandmother was cremated. She has said goodbye to her dear Gran for the last time, but she can't yet accept the fact that she will never see her again. Her memories are still fresh – she can feel the warmth of her grandmother's fingers and hear her voice. She will gradually get over it, once she understands that everyone has to die. Her grandmother died when her life was completed. She became old and passed away naturally."

Anna did not want to change the subject altogether – that would be too insensitive – but she wanted to help Sikha. So she asked: "What happens at a Hindu funeral?"

Mr Datta said, "Hindus do not bury their dead. They burn them, on specially built funeral pyres to which sandalwood is added. The fire is kindled by pouring ghee (clarified butter) on the pyre. Incense is added as the flames consume the body. In India, Hindus prefer to be cremated on the banks of the Ganges, into which their bones and ashes may be thrown. People who live a long way from the Ganges perform the ceremony on the banks of any river. Sometimes, where there are no rivers, relatives of the deceased carry the ashes long distances to the Ganges. They believe that the Ganges, our holy river, will carry the dead person's soul to heaven."

"Do British Hindus ever do that?"

"I believe some do," said Mr Datta. "Here the body is put in a coffin and taken to the crematorium, where it rests on a conveyor at the entrance to the furnace. Prayers connected with the funeral rites are said by the priest. Condolence messages are read, events from the life of the deceased and his or her qualities are recalled, and their last wishes are remembered by the relatives and friends who have gathered at the chapel. Then, at the appropriate moment, when the funeral pyre would be lit, a few burning incense sticks are touched to the coffin by the eldest son or the closest relative. This act is called the **mukhagni**. The conveyor is switched on and the coffin slowly passes into the furnace.

"Afterwards, a handful of ash is collected in a container and returned to the relatives. This is sometimes taken to be thrown into the Thames or flown to India, I believe. In London, the Hindu Centre can make all the necessary arrangements."

"The body must burn very quickly!" said Sikha, frowning.

"Yes. It is all over in a matter of a few minutes," Mr Datta replied thoughtfully. "Our earthly frame of flesh and blood, which

Funeral procession arriving at the pyre where the body will be burnt

has been cared for since birth, a body that was recognized as a human being, a person, is suddenly reduced to mere ashes. Only the memories of our actions survive, and they, too, will be forgotten in time."

"But Hindus believe that the soul of a person never dies," Goutam remarked. Nobody had noticed him come in.

"That is correct," Mr Datta said. "According to the sacred Bhagwat Gita, the soul simply moves to a new body, just as we discard our clothes and change into new ones. We worry about death because of our ties with our present life, but if we recognize our inner self – the soul – death is nothing to worry about, really. It is like going to sleep at the end of a long and tiring day. Eternal sleep.

"There are, however, many rites to be performed. For ten days following a death, the members of the family observe **asoucha**, which means that they consider themselves unclean. During this period they do not cut their hair or nails, or shave, and the person who performed the mukhagni must not wear a stitched garment, such as a shirt, or shoes. He also wears an iron key on a cotton thread round his neck."

"Why?" asked Sikha.

"To ward off the spirit of the dead person. It is believed that the departed soul assumes its next form during this period, but only a tenth part each day. Ceremonial rites are performed to assist it. While it is growing, the soul looks for a body to go into in its next form. It may become impatient and choose to return to a living person, especially to one of those who took part in the cremation rites. This may be harmful to the person.

"After the tenth day but within a month of the cremation, on a day which is both auspicious and convenient to the family, the **shraddha** ceremony is performed. This ceremony is almost as important as the marriage ceremony, and can be just as expensive. It is a feast held in honour of the departed soul, now in its new but frail form and in need of nourishment. Again, elaborate rituals surround the feast, including bathing and shaving for all those related to the deceased."

"Will you tell us about one or two other rituals, please?" Anna asked.

"You must find them quite fascinating!" Mr Datta commented. "And they are fascinating," he agreed, "once you know the meaning behind them. There is one called **pindadaan**. It entails offering rice-balls to the spirit of the dead. The eldest son or a near relative of the deceased prepares ten such balls, mixing uncooked rice, grapes, ghee, honey and milk or yoghurt. The rite is performed with reverence, taking care that the procedure is carried out to the letter as prescribed in the Vedas. As usual, many other rites are performed, the priest conducting the performer through them.

"The family of the deceased are expected to be generous at this time. Gifts are freely given and the Brahmins in particular are honoured, at a special feast. This is called 'Brahman Bhojan', 'feeding the Brahmins'. Depending on the status of the family, these gifts could be cash, utensils (such as a brass cooking-pot), furniture or even gold. Besides offering gifts people also like to donate money to a charity or to a good cause in the name of the deceased," Mr Datta added.

"One of our uncles once went somewhere to perform a ceremony called **gangasthi**," Goutam recalled. "Can you tell us about it, please?" he asked his father.

Mr Datta exclaimed, "Good Heavens! I'm amazed you remembered that! Yes, it was when my aunt died that her eldest son went to the holy city of Hardwar on the banks of the Ganges, carrying his mother's bones. The word 'gangasthi' is made up of two words: ganga (the Ganges), and asthi (bones). Thus the ceremony is that of casting the bones into the Ganges.

"On the third day after the cremation," continued Mr Datta, "accompanied by the priest, the relatives return to the cremation ground to collect a few bones from the site of the funeral pyre, and a bone-gathering ceremony is performed. The bones are placed in an urn. Later on, on a suitable day determined by the priest, the bones are taken to the Ganges. This rite is performed within a year of death."

"Why did your cousin go to that particular city?" Anna asked.

"Because the three cities of Hardwar, Varanashi and Gaya are considered the holiest of all the cities along the Ganges. There, on the ghats, or steps on the river-bank, literally hundreds of Brahmins can be seen performing these rites. As I mentioned earlier, in Britain a handful of ashes, rather than bones, is given to the relatives after the cremation so that they can scatter them."

"What about the shraddha ceremony in this country, Daddy?" asked Sikha.

Burning ghat on the Ganges at Varanashi (Benares)

"There is absolutely no problem with that," Mr Datta said. "It can be performed in a community hall or even at home. The Hindu Centre is frequently used for this purpose. There are many professional Hindu priests in Britain today who will advise on all aspects of Hindu ceremonies, and perform them for a fee.

"Finally, I would like to recall the thoughts expressed by the great Rabindra Nath Tagore in one of his poems:

> Unknown to death, I tremble with its fear,
> My eyes fill with tears to part with my world.
> With both hands I cling on to 'life' as mine
> Yet, who I ask made this world, this life belong to me
> Even before my birth?
> At dawn of death the Unknown's familiar face
>   is glimpsed,
> I have loved my life as I have lived
> So will I love death as I die."

"How very profound," said Goutam.

Anna agreed. "I would like to learn it by heart so that I could say it to Sumitra. I am sure she would find much comfort in those words."

"Not just yet," said Mr Datta gently. "Maybe later on, when there is peace in her mind and she can remember her grandmother without pain. Then the poet's words will make her feel that her gran is still close to her and, wherever she may be, she is happy."

14
Saraswati Puja

Mrs Saunders, Head of R.E. at Heathurst School, was surprised when Anna approached her with a special request. It was a letter from her parents, seeking permission for her to attend **Saraswati Puja** with the Dattas.

"But that's a Hindu festival!" she said.

"I know, Mrs Saunders. That is why I would like to go. I've been to several Hindu festivals already, but this one takes place during school hours. I am learning about Hindu festivals and customs because I think it's important to understand something of different faiths. May I go, Mrs Saunders?" she asked eagerly.

"Of course you may. I'm glad you are so interested."

Saraswati is the goddess of learning and the arts. She is the wife of Brahma, the Creator. Saraswati Puja takes place on the fifth day after the new moon in the month of Magha, the tenth month of the Hindu calendar.

Mrs Datta and her children picked up Anna on their way to Greenford, where the puja was being held at a friend's house. According to the Bengali tradition, the goddess is very popular with students, especially schoolchildren, who sincerely believe that with her blessings they will learn well and be successful in their careers.

Several families were already there when they arrived. Mrs Datta had brought some fresh flowers, sweets and other things for the puja. The younger children were playing upstairs. Anna and Sikha offered to help the women with the final arrangements. The **Naivedya**, the offerings to the deity – rice, fruit, flowers, etc. – were beautifully arranged on separate plates according to shape, size and colour.

As the auspicious moment approached Mr Mukerji, the priest conducting the ceremony, called the house to order. Then he

The goddess Saraswati

invoked the gods by ringing a bell. As the invocation of the deities continued, he proceeded with all the rituals of the puja. Everyone sat round watching the worship, looking up at the beautiful pith image of Saraswati now and then. Even the smallest children sat still and watched. Then it was time for the **Pushpanjali**: Mr Mukerji asked them all to come forward and offer their prayers to the goddess with flowers.

Afterwards they all shared the delicious cooked prasaad of khichuri (rice and pulses), aloo-kapi (spiced potato and cauliflower) and chutni (tomato and plum chutney), all prepared by Mrs Mukerji and her friends.

Anna wanted to know if the puja is held in every household. Mrs Datta explained, "No, but several families get together and organize a joint celebration. It is not a public holiday as such – in India, only the schools are closed. A lot of people who are at work during the day, including my husband, will be here this evening to see the arati – the prayer to the goddess with the five-branched lamp. We are here now so that our children can attend the puja at the right moment and, more important, for the Pushpanjali."

"I was very impressed by the way the children said their prayers, and by their behaviour!" Anna remarked. "I, too, felt as if I was communicating with the goddess when I looked at Saraswati during the puja," she added.

Sikha congratulated her. "If that's how you felt, you are bound to do well in your exams," she told her. "Have faith in Saraswati."

15
Why Britain?

The record had finished, but the magic of Pannalal's flute recital had mesmerized everyone. At last Anna broke the silence.

"Excuse me, Mr Datta," she said softly.

"Yes, Anna?" Mr Datta's eyes were closed. He was obviously still absorbed in the music.

"Well," she began shyly, "I was watching you while you were listening to that music. Your thoughts had travelled far away! I was wondering whether you miss India. I'd also like to know what made you decide to come to Britain, rather than another country."

"My dear Anna," he said, "yes, there are times when I miss the life I enjoyed in my younger days. As for your second question, well, I chose to come here because I was attracted by England from an early age. The most important thing to remember is that I did not come to Britain under any kind of pressure," he continued. "Many of my contemporaries also came here, following the example of some of the famous Indians who had preceded us. As young students we read their biographies. We learned about their achievements and their experiences abroad and took an interest in everything that happened in Britain. Secretly, we longed to visit England some day, to expand our horizons."

"Who were those famous people?" Anna enquired.

"Vivekananda, Sri Aurobindo, Subhas Bose, Gandhi, Nehru and Dr Radhakrishnan, for example. There were many others, but these are the names from my personal album of the 'most famous'. As it happened, all of them were Hindus who did a great deal to make the Western world aware of our religion, philosophy and culture." Mr Datta's eyes were shining. He obviously felt very proud that those great names were his Hindu compatriots.

"I'm afraid I've only heard of Gandhi and Nehru," Anna said.

"Probably because they were great political leaders," replied Mr

117

Datta. "But Vivekananda was the first Hindu missionary ever to preach Hinduism in the West. He went to the World Parliament of Religions in Chicago in 1893 and delivered a totally unprepared speech. He spoke as if inspired by Saraswati's blessings. With his powerful speech he captivated the vast crowd in the Hall of Columbus, and with the first five words of his opening address, 'Sisters and brothers of America', he won their hearts. He preached that the greatest and the noblest effort is that which is made for the service of mankind. From America he came to England."

"But why England?" Anna interrupted.

"I'll have to run through some history to explain that," smiled Mr Datta. "India's links with England are nearly four hundred years old, but it was in the second half of the eighteenth century and during the nineteenth century that the influence of the West, and particularly of Britain, began to spread in India. The British had set up their administrative headquarters in Bengal and engaged many local people to work in their offices. Indians everywhere wanted to learn English. Gradually, through the untiring efforts of great British missionaries like William Carey and the Reverend Duff, English began to be taught in schools.

Government House, Calcutta, the British administrative centre in India

"As Western education spread it brought about a significant change in people's way of thinking. They were becoming more and more progressive. They started to question traditional beliefs and values. Also, within a span of nine years – between 1863 and 1872 – three great sons of Mother India were born, two in Bengal and one in Gujarat. These men were to change the course of Indian history."

"Who were they, Daddy?" Sikha asked.

"Why, Vivekananda and Aurobindo in Bengal and Gandhi in Gujarat, of course," replied Mr Datta. "By then, such was the impact of Western education that Aurobindo was sent to Cambridge at a very early age to be educated and Gandhi came to London to study Law. He was called to the Bar at the Inner Temple. Nehru was educated at Harrow and later at Cambridge. Subhas C. Bose, known as 'Netaji', 'The Leader', also went to Cambridge."

"Tagore also came to England to study, but returned to India before completing his education," Goutam recalled.

Rabindra Nath Tagore in 1921

Jawaharlal Nehru at Harrow

"Was Cambridge very popular with Indian students?" Anna asked innocently.

"I knew I couldn't escape that question! I have mentioned the university three times, haven't I?" Mr Datta laughed. "No, it was just a coincidence. The great Dr Radhakrishnan, for example, was associated with Oxford. He was Professor of Eastern Religion and Philosophy there for nearly sixteen years!"

"What about Indian women?" Goutam asked.

"I am glad you asked me that. The women were severely restricted in those days. Very few went to school or received formal education until social reformers and educationists like Vidyasagar and Raja Ram Mohan Roy spoke out on their behalf. Then women began to be educated as well. As a schoolboy I was attracted by the poems of Sarojini Naidu, and later by the personality and the achievements of Nehru's sister, Vijayalakshmi Pandit. She held many distinguished posts, including a term of office as High Commissioner to Britain that ended just before I arrived here.

Vijayalakshmi Pandit and Krishna Menon, whom she succeeded as Indian High Commissioner, on their way to the London Suez Conference, 1952

"There was another interesting development," continued Mr Datta. "These highly educated Indians studied the form of government in India and became conscious of the many drawbacks of the administration. A sense of nationalism, and a desire for self-rule, to break free of foreign domination, was growing in them. Many British people were becoming critical of their role in India too. Dr Annie Besant, a religious scholar and thinker who lived in India for many years, even helped the Indians in their struggle for independence, and became President of the Indian National Congress!

"As a small boy I had seen the sudden change that came about in India in 1947, when the country became independent, and in the following year, when Gandhi was assassinated. I became aware of his great contribution to the world, but only after he died! While learning about all these events taking place all around me, I too, without realizing it, was being drawn towards English literature. When I left school I went on to higher education, and met more people who had been to England, mostly teachers at the university. My desire to visit England grew stronger. There were also many doctors, engineers and civil servants who had finished their training abroad and returned to India to work. ... I hope you can now see that my decision to come to Britain was not made on the spur of the moment. A young man's dream, it grew over many years and had to be achieved."

"Did you find everything just as you had expected when you first arrived in Britain?" Anna asked.

"Not quite," Mr Datta replied. "Naturally, I felt a bit lost until I made some friends. Then I realized that in Britain there were people from almost every part of India and from every religion. Practically all of us had gone through the same thought-process while deciding to come to Britain. Some had come because England offered greater scope for building a successful career. Others had travelled first to Germany, with a restricted work permit.

"In Britain, our common identity was 'Indian' and our common language, English! Most of us were students, either full-time or part-time, and most of us planned to return to India after finishing our studies. We used to meet at India House or at the India League in Aldwych. But gradually, missing the important religious celebrations of our respective regions of India, we began to search

122

Dr Annie Besant with the philosopher and teacher J. Krishnamurti

out our own community or religious groups. We came together first as Hindus, then as Bengalis, to celebrate Durga Puja at Hampstead Town Hall or Saraswati Puja at the Friends' House in Euston. Occasionally we went to the Ramakrishna Mission at Dukes Avenue in Muswell Hill.

"Our other meeting-places were to be the Commonwealth Institute, which opened in 1962, and the Hindu Centre, which opened in the same year. In 1962 the first Commonwealth Immigrants Act was passed, too."

"What was that?" Sikha asked.

"Well, in 1948 a British Nationality Law came into force. This law declared the citizens of India to be 'citizens of the United Kingdom and Colonies' and as such they had the right to come and live in Britain. But by 1962 so many people had arrived from the 'new' Commonwealth countries that an Act was passed to limit the number of job vouchers issued each year to people entering Britain. India had been independent for only fifteen years, yet we were already coming under pressure. All of a sudden, there

The Commonwealth Institute

124

was a new aspect to our common identity: Indians were now regarded as a minority group!"

"As a Hindu, do you see any change in society or in people's attitudes today?" Anna asked.

"Oh yes!" Mr Datta said emphatically. "The political changes in East African countries forced thousands of Hindus to leave their African homes and come to Britain, especially between 1968 and 1975. Whole families came and settled in London, Leicester, Bradford, Leeds, Coventry, Manchester and other cities. Their children joined local schools. At school these Hindu children grew up with other children from all over the world. The Hindus are a hard-working people. They set up shops in the high streets and opened businesses. They also formed religious societies and opened temples for worship.

"The sudden increase in their number has given the Hindus more confidence to practise their faith and to keep their customs within a Western society and gain its respect. Now the multi-ethnic character of British society is recognized in all spheres and at all levels. The very fact that you are with us today, Anna, trying to learn about our culture and our way of life, shows that a change has come about. More and more young people are becoming interested in each other's culture and religion.

"But Hinduism is complex. It has so many aspects that it can confuse those who are not familiar with its practices. There are so many communities, so many languages, so many customs and so many people interpreting Hinduism in so many different ways – each according to his or her own understanding and conviction. It is all too easy to miss the essentially Hindu element while looking at a particular community's way of life. ... Does that answer your questions?" Mr Datta asked Anna kindly.

"Yes, of course. Thank you. It was a wonderful history lesson," Anna replied with a smile.

16
A Wedding

The wedding! Anna arrived at the Dattas' house very early, but Goutam was already loading up the car with a tray of gifts and a brass container of which a lot of fuss was being made. Anna wondered whether it held holy water from the Ganges, but she learned afterwards that it was turmeric paste. Anil had been smeared with the paste the day before. Later, as he washed it off, some had been collected. Now this was being sent in advance to the bride's home, where it would be mixed with turmeric paste specially prepared for Gouri for a similar ritual. This rite is known as **gayey holood**, "turmeric on the body".

Sikha called Anna aside. "Come upstairs," she said. "There's something I'd like to show you."

"But this is Goutam's room!" Anna stopped outside the door.

Sikha laughed and said, "It was! He has lost it to Anil, just for this week. Now come in, and be quick."

"My word! What has happened?" Anna couldn't believe her eyes. The room had been transformed into a bridal chamber!

"You see, our house is being used as the bridegroom's house and the one in Barnet as the bride's," explained Sikha. "After the wedding the couple will return here."

"And this will be their bedroom."

"That's right. But it isn't quite ready. On the third night after the wedding there will be flowers all over the room. Even the bed, the first they share as a married couple, will be strewn with petals. The custom is called **phoolsajya**, 'bed of flowers'."

Downstairs, what looked like a fashion parade of dazzling saris and jewellery filled every room. Everyone was bubbling with excitement. Sikha told Anna they were waiting for the **shubha-yatra** to begin.

"What's that?" asked Anna.

"It simply means 'auspicious journey'. It's when the groom and his party set off for the wedding."

Anil looked handsome and elegant in a silk kurta and a dhoti with a tightly pleated border, like the edge of a fan. A line of four-pointed stars decorated his forehead and on his feet were lightweight white slippers. He held a crown-like pith cap called a **topor** decorated with the daintiest of sculptured patterns.

"Those tiny stars on his forehead were made by dipping the head of a clove in sandalwood paste," Sikha told her friend.

"Really? I would never have guessed," replied Anna.

Anil was flanked by his father and his uncle. A small boy stood close to him, dressed to look like a miniature bridegroom.

"Who is the little boy?" giggled Anna. "He looks like a mascot!"

"He is the **nit-bor**, or **kol-bor**, which means 'lap bridegroom'," Goutam answered. "You are quite right. He is like a mascot – a comic figure dressed up like a proper bridegroom. The groom's party is never complete without a nit-bor."

Decorated car waiting to take the bridegroom to his wedding, Orissa

127

The shubha-yatra began. Destination: Hampstead Town Hall. As he drove, Mr Datta explained, "Traditionally the party comprised only men, but these days women are included. Both families are having to make certain compromises in order to keep the social and official formalities. For example, in Britain, for the sake of convenience most marriages are held on a Saturday (which may not be the most auspicious day) and a hall must be hired for the weekend. In order to coincide with the most auspicious time of day in India – **godhuli lagna**, the 'moment of cattle-dust' (dusk) – the wedding is taking place in the early afternoon. I wonder if you realize, Anna, that officially the wedding is already over?"

"What do you mean?"

"By law every marriage has to be legalized at a Register Office, you see. Yesterday Anil and Gouri exchanged their marriage vows in the presence of the Superintendent Registrar, with two friends as witnesses. Their names were entered in the register as husband and wife and they were issued a certificate. What you will see today is the 'proper' wedding, according to our social and religious customs."

"Did you say that the cost of the reception is being shared by both families, Dad?" asked Goutam.

"Yes, that is correct. In India all the arrangements for today would have been the responsibility of the bride's parents."

"That is the same for most Christian marriages, too, I think," remarked Anna, "but it doesn't seem right. Surely the bride-groom's parents should contribute as well?" Sikha nodded in agreement.

Mr Datta laughed. "How nice it is to be in the company of such fair-minded people! Well, in India another reception dinner is given in honour of the bride when she arrives at her father-in-law's house. It is called **bou-bhaat**, 'the bride's feast'. This, too, is a big affair and it is the responsibility of the bridegroom's family."

"Good!" said the girls, smiling.

When the car pulled up by the steps of the town hall, Anna was startled to hear a strange noise being made by a chorus of women.

Goutam explained, "That's called **uloodhyani**. Dhyani means 'sound'. The repeated *uloo* is produced by quivering the tongue around the lips to distort a sharp *oo* sound."

"Why are they doing it?" asked Anna.

"According to our custom the womenfolk make this noise to

announce an auspicious and a happy event. In this case it is for the arrival of the bridegroom."

Anil quickly put on his wedding-cap and helped the little boy with his. A lot of people had lined the stairs to watch.

"Another fashion parade!" whispered Goutam. "Only ten times bigger!" His cheeky remark got him a sharp dig in the ribs from Sikha.

A recording of shanai music played in the background. Anna recognized the tune. The hall looked most impressive. It had been decorated with lights, flowers and oriental cut-out patterns. On the stage a high platform had been built under a colourful canopy. Red and silver glittered everywhere under the lights.

Anil and the little nit-bor were ushered by the ladies to a seat on the dais. The blessing rites were performed, and Anil was given a gold ring. He was then helped to stand on a **shila**, a stone slab, for another ritual. The ladies washed his feet and touched his shoulders and forehead with a basket containing several objects.

Bride and groom being welcomed by the priest before their wedding, London. The groom wears a Punjabi head-dress with a veil.

129

"This is a welcoming ceremony called **baran**," Mr Datta said. "He is being treated like a human god."

Suddenly, there was another burst of uloodhyani.

"The bride!" A ripple of excitement passed through the crowd. Gouri looked like an eastern queen! She was decked in jewellery from head to toe and wore a dazzling, bright-red sari. Anna drew closer to have a good look. The brocade of the sari rustled at every movement and the silver ankle-bells jingled at each step she took.

"That sari is made of Benares silk and the elaborate patterns are woven in gold and silver thread," Sikha whispered.

Gouri walked forward slowly, holding a betel leaf over her eyes. Her brother and a friend helped her. Then, as Anil stood on the stone slab, she walked round him in a circle seven times.

Mr Datta explained, "At the right moment she will remove the leaf and look straight into the bridegroom's eyes. This is called **shubha-dristi**, the 'holy exchange of eye'. Now the bride and groom are exchanging garlands."

"Does that mean the wedding is over?" Anna asked.

"Oh no!" laughed Mr Datta. "The Hindu wedding ceremony is long and elaborate. This is only a preliminary rite, although a very significant one."

The couple sat down in front of the urn for the sacred fire, the **Agni**, and the priest began to recite verses.

Gouri's father took his seat. He was to give his daughter away. First he offered Anil a little water from a small boat-shaped dish to refresh himself. Anil accepted some. Then he was offered a mixture of honey and ghee. He accepted that too, saying, "All my dealings in life will be refined with the sweetness of honey." This rite is called **madhuparka**.

"Why is the priest wrapping their hands together?" Anna asked.

Mr Datta explained, "The clay pitcher in front of the couple is holy. The priest places Gouri's right hand on top of Anil's, palms together. He winds a cloth with five different dried fruits in its folds round their joined hands and ties them up with a garland of flowers. Their hands rest on the pitcher.

"Gouri's father holds her shoulder-wrap with his left hand and with his right he touches the sacred bowl of water. He then introduces himself, the bridegroom and the bride and declares that he hands his daughter over to Anil.

"Traditionally, the couple put on a new set of clothes and

130

discard their old ones at this point in the ceremony. To suit the present-day taste, however, the bride and groom simply accept the gifts of clothes offered to them."

"The sacred fire is being lit!" Anna observed.

"Yes," said Mr Datta. "In India a pit would have been prepared in the floor, but here a small fire is being lit inside a metal urn. The priest recites from the Vedas and a lot of fragrant herbs and incense are burnt. The fire is kindled to strengthen the bond of love and to destroy all selfish desires. The offering to the sacred fire is called **homa**. With his finger, the priest takes a smear of the soot mixed with oil and puts a holy spot on the forehead of the bride and groom. Then, using his ring, Anil draws a line of vermilion in the parting of Gouri's hair."

"Oh yes," interrupted Anna, "Mrs Datta told me that the vermilion mark was the sign of a married woman."

"That's right. The couple will now perform an important ceremony," continued Mr Datta. "They will vow to remain true to each other as good partners in life and to do everything in their power to uphold the traditions of both their families for their mutual happiness and prosperity."

"Look — they're doing something to Gouri's feet!" Anna pointed out excitedly.

"That is her brother," said Mr Datta. "He is trying to place her right foot on the stone slab. The ritual of standing on the stone is performed so that the bride may remain steady as a rock through life's ups and downs. In his left hand Gouri's brother has a basket of puffed rice. Gouri will hold out her hands, palm upwards, to receive some of the rice, and will then cast it into the fire. This act is repeated four times, with Anil following her as she walks round the sacred fire. Now Gouri takes her seat on Anil's left. A corner of her sari is knotted to the end of Anil's shoulder-wrap."

"They are going somewhere."

"Only to the next patch of floor," said Mr Datta, "to perform yet another ritual. This one is called **saptapadi,** meaning 'seven steps'. Anil and Gouri will take seven steps into their life together: the first for mutual support, the second for strength, the third for prosperity, the fourth for everlasting peace of mind and stability, the fifth for children, the sixth for the six seasons and the seventh for loyalty and companionship."

"Did you say six seasons? asked Anna, puzzled.

131

The clothes of the bride and groom are tied together to symbolize their union.

"Yes, we have six seasons in India: Grishma (Summer), Varsha (Rainy), Sarat (Autumn), Hemant (Dewy), Sheeth (Winter) and Vasant (Spring)."

"Are there any more rituals in the wedding ceremony?"

"Just a few. As he repeats the verses said by the priest, Anil points upwards to show his wife the radiance of the sun and the steadfastness of the Pole Star. They also make a gesture of touching each other's hearts, which means that their two hearts are now one. Then the priest sprinkles the couple with holy water. The wedding ceremony is now complete and the elders are coming forward to bless the couple. If you will excuse me for a minute, I will join them."

"Of course, Mr Datta," said Anna. She quickly took a picture of him as he gave his blessings to the couple.

After the wedding there was a magnificent dinner. Mr Datta told Anna, "You'd better stay close to me, and remember the golden rules. Round one – try a little bit of everything but don't forget the combination: dal, dry spiced vegetables and deep-fried fish or vegetables, a twist of lemon and a bite of chilli. Round two: meat or fish, salad... ." Mr Datta scanned the table. "Yes, there it is! Round three: chutni and rice, and then you'll be ready for the final course: the sweets. And sweets there are many! The Guptas of Hendon, who are doing the catering, have supplied this wedding very well. This is dil-khus (heart's delight) and that's chamchom, a firm sponge soaked with syrup. There is rasogolla, too, which has always been a challenge to your self-control."

Anna laughed as a very happy Mr Datta went on tempting her with all those delicious dishes.

On their way to Barnet Mr Datta explained, "The town hall was used as an extension to the bride's home. One or two amusing ceremonies will be performed at Barnet. All through the night the bridegroom is put through a mocking session."

"A mocking session?" Anna was surprised, and curious.

"Oh yes," Mr Datta said with a glint in his eye. "The poor bridegroom is surrounded by a hostile crowd, females out-numbering males, and subjected to all sorts of pranks and insults. Someone will hide a cowrie shell in the folds of the bride's sari in her lap and ask the groom to find it. Thinking that this is the custom, the groom will make a serious effort to look for the shell.

133

While struggling he has to swallow embarrassing remarks like: 'Oh, you are useless!' 'Look at you – searching through a lady's sari for a silly cowrie shell!' and so on."

"Any more?" asked Anna, laughing.

"Of course!" Mr Datta replied obligingly. "The bride will be given a betel-nut to hold tightly and the groom must try to take it from her. Now, if he is too gentle, for fear of hurting his bride's fingers, he will be called a weakling and a drip. If, on the other hand, he applies a little pressure, they will call him a beast and a brute."

Anna was still giggling. "But it is so silly!" she protested.

Mr Datta agreed. "That's the whole idea! Anyway, the night passes. Very few people sleep. The following morning the bride sets off on her journey to her husband's home. It is a touching moment when the daughter of the family goes round taking leave of all her near and dear ones. There are many who cannot bear this moment. The bride's mother's eyes fill with tears and she moves away to dry them. It is considered inauspicious to shed tears at this moment, but very few mothers can hide their emotions.

"Tomorrow Gouri and Anil will leave for our house. On their arrival there will be a few welcoming rituals. Gouri will be asked to hold a pitcher of water. A pot of milk will be heated and if it boils over as she enters the household it is supposed to be an auspicious omen. A handful of rice is always thrown over the bride's head and she may even be asked to hold a live fish – usually a slippery trout!"

"Why?" Anna frowned.

"Just for fun, to prove that her grip is firm and that she is well-versed in all the domestic chores. Many young wives squeamishly let the wriggling fish slip through their fingers and are teased. I think Gouri will manage it. She is a doctor – besides, I shall not be too pleased if she drops it on my carpet!"

"Oh! Mr Datta!"

He laughed and continued, "Tomorrow is also the night when the couple part company and sleep in separate quarters. On the third day after the wedding a big feast is held, as I have already explained. In this case we will have about fifty or sixty guests. Then the couple will spend the night as a married couple.

"You see, each wedding is different. Athough the basic principles are observed according to the Vedic Rules, local customs

134

differ quite a lot. The rituals also vary from one community to the next. So you won't see a universal pattern in all Hindu weddings if you only follow the rituals. I think that we all did our best today, but I cannot guarantee that the rites performed conformed to the traditional rules. In Britain, the weather, the expense and lack of time are bound to impose restrictions. However, if both the families are satisfied and Anil and Gouri are happy in life, then nothing else matters."

"I agree," Anna said emphatically and concluded, "I enjoyed every minute of it."

The newly married couple sitting on the bed of flowers. The bride's pith-work head-dress is similar to that worn by the groom during the wedding ceremony.

QUESTIONS AND PROJECTS

Chapters 12–16

1 In India, the illuminations are the main attraction of Divali. Describe a festival from another faith in which light or fire plays a part.

2 The Hindus believe that the soul of a person never dies. Do you agree?

3 Make a study of the funeral rites of two or more religions.

4 Saraswati is the goddess of learning and the arts, Lakshmi is the goddess of prosperity and Ganesha is the god of wisdom and success. Find out about the Christian tradition of patron saints. For example, to which saints might dentists, firemen or musicians pray?

5 Would you be happy to travel in order to improve your work prospects? What would you most miss about your area or about Britain if you moved away?

6 What were the political changes that took place in Africa between 1968 and 1975 and forced many Hindu families to come to Britain?

7 Write a short account of the life and work of two of the following: Mahatma Gandhi, Pandit Nehru, Indira Gandhi, Sri Aurobindo, Subhas Bose, Dr Radhakrishnan, Rabindra Nath Tagore.

8 Find out about wedding ceremonies in faiths other than Hinduism. What similarities and differences are there?

9 Choose three different religions and draw the traditional wedding clothes worn by the bride and the groom in each case.

17
Holi

About a fortnight after the wedding an outing was arranged to the Hindu temple at Letchmore Heath, near Watford. They had just driven over the Brent Cross flyover when Mr Datta asked, "Why is everybody so quiet today?"

"They're probably wondering what to expect when we arrive!" Mrs Datta smiled.

"I don't even know where you are taking me," grumbled Anna. "All I know is that we're going to another festival."

"Aha! It's supposed to be a surprise!" Sikha teased her.

"It had better be a good one."

"It will, it will," said Goutam with a wicked grin.

After a while they drove through a village and turned off the road into the grounds of the huge country house.

"This is the temple, Anna," said Mrs Datta.

"What a place!" she exclaimed. "Is it really a temple? Was it bought through donations? It must have cost a fortune!"

"No, it wasn't bought at all," replied Mr Datta. "The entire manor was donated to the International Society of Krishna Consciousness, which has branches all over Britain."

"Goodness!" Anna was amazed. "Whoever donated it must be as rich as a king!"

Mr Datta told her, "Probably not as rich as a Maharaja, but certainly more famous. It was George Harrison, the former Beatle. The devotees of Lord Krishna have turned the house into a temple. The daily programme is much more elaborate here than at the Hindu Centre.

"The arati, or worship, takes place several times a day, with a different set of rituals each time. The first arati is at half past four in the morning. The programme is even more elaborate on

137

*A member of the International Society of Krishna Consciousness
(ISKCON) preaching at the Rath Yatra festival in Trafalgar Square*

An ISKCON member shares a joke with a holy man.

Sundays, with video-shows, drama, children's classes, hymn-singing and so on. The devotees hold talks and discussions and receive visitors ranging from members of the Police Training College to pupils from various schools. Prasaad is distributed after the puja."

When they entered the temple, Anna and her friends were cordially received by the saffron-clad devotees of Lord Krishna, who joined their hands and greeted them saying "Hare Krishna".

Inside there were the most beautiful images of Lord Krishna and his consort, Radha, that Anna had ever seen. The deities were lavishly adorned with jewellery and the whole building was beautifully decorated and spotlessly clean.

It was a glorious day, and quite warm too, so they decided to go out and wander in the grounds of the temple. A lot of people were already doing just that. A bonfire had been lit. Some people were going round the fire and throwing coconuts and other offerings into it and singing songs of Krishna to the accompaniment of cymbals and drums.

Suddenly Sikha produced a little cardboard box, dipped her hand into it, took a handful of bright red powder and smeared Anna's face with it! Poor girl! She was so taken aback that she could only say, "Oh no! Why?" She was also beginning to look cross. The idea that it was meant to be fun began to sink in when Sikha did the same to Goutam. Then they both got hold of Mrs

139

Datta, and she fared no better. Next they all turned on Mr Datta. He had already begun to run, but his head start was no match for the speed of the youngsters. Moments later he was wiping his glasses, his face a lovely red!

Mrs Datta explained to Anna that it was **Holi**, the Festival of Colour. In India they would probably have spent the whole day spraying and smearing each other with lots and lots of different colours.

"There are so many different ways of throwing colour at people, too!" she said. "There are spray-guns, coloured powders and coloured water and special sprays, popularly known as 'vanishing colours', for attacking colleagues at work. These do not damage or stain clothes and evaporate quickly. Over here one cannot take such liberties, unfortunately. It is a different story altogether in the tropical sun."

After hearing all this, Anna picked up a box of the red powder and said threateningly, "So this is the surprise you were planning! You rotten lot! Wait till I get you!"

Both Sikha and Goutam picked themselves up and ran for their lives, but Sikha was soon on the ground. She couldn't outrun Anna, but Goutam did. Anna chased him for quite a while. When she eventually caught him, she realized that the music had stopped and all the people who had been dancing round the bonfire were now watching them!

One of the devotees invited them all to come back inside and said how delighted they were to see a family enjoying the great festival of Holi. They washed their hands and faces and sat down to have some cooked prasaad. Afterwards there were prayers and then they watched a play from the life of Lord Krishna.

On the way back Mrs Datta told Anna more about the festival. Holi may have started as a harvest festival. It marks the end of winter and the beginning of spring. It takes place on the day of the full moon in Phalguna, the eleventh month of the Hindu calendar. People enjoy themselves by playing tricks on each other and throwing coloured water and making fools of themselves. It is a remarkable occasion which breaks down the barriers of faith, caste and status. Bonfires are lit to burn the effigy of Holika, the sorceress who took her young nephew Prahlad, a great devotee of Vishnu, into a blazing fire to destroy him. He survived, but Holika perished in the flames!

140

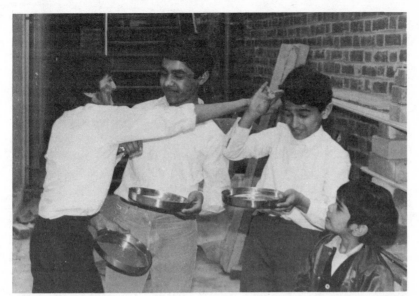

Children smearing each other with red powder (Hindu Temple, Southall)

Eighteenth-century painting of villagers spraying coloured water at Holi

18
Naba Barsha: New Year

Scarcely four weeks had passed since the fun and games of Holi when Anna received a beautiful New Year card from the Dattas. It was handmade, with the portrait of a farm-girl painted on a dried pipul leaf and mounted on a dark brown card. The message read: "Greetings of **Naba Barsha** – Happy New Year from all of us". At first she thought it was a joke. "But they have all signed," she said to herself.

She looked at the calendar to make sure it really was 14 April, and then picked up the phone. Mr Datta answered.

"Thank you for the very beautiful card, but I am all confused. How can it be New Year's Day when Sumitra's father said that it was New Year's Day on Divali?" Anna enquired.

Mr Datta laughed and said, "Don't forget that the customs in western and eastern India vary a lot. Today is the first day of Baisakh. It's the Bengali New Year's Day. We follow a different

New Year card with a picture of stick-dancers in a Gujarati village

calendar to that of the western parts of India. In the streets of Bengal, people go out in a procession singing and welcoming the New Year. It is a great social occasion. We have displays of singing and dancing everywhere and friends visit each other's families.

"My wife has cooked some delicious dishes and we are having a few friends round early this afternoon. Why not come over and have a New Year feast with us?"

Anna replied, "Honestly, Mr Datta! How you spoil me! You do know my weakness for your cooking, and you take full advantage of it! Thank you so much, anyway, and Happy New Year!"

THE HINDU CALENDAR

The Hindu calendar is a lunar one, worked out from the waxing and waning of the moon, whereas the Western calendar is calculated from the position of the sun. The Dattas follow a Bengali calendar and their year begins with Baisakh. The months or 'maash' are as follows:

Baisakh (April–May)
Jaistha (May–June)
Asada (June–July)
Shravana (July–August)
Bhadra (August–September)
Aswin (September–October)
Kartik (October–November)
Agrahayan (November–December)
Pausha (December–January)
Magha (January–February)
Phalguna (February–March)
Chaitra (March–April)

19
Contrasting Cultures

It was a glorious Sunday afternoon in July. The Dattas had been working hard since morning to get the house back in order. The day before, they had entertained nearly forty people (including Anna) who came to participate in the **Satyanarayan Puja**.

When Anna arrived they were relaxing in the garden, sitting on the soft green lawn which was Mr Datta's pride and joy. Anna had become a regular visitor and the Dattas treated her like a member of the family.

"Hello, Anna. You must find the house a bit quiet today," said Goutam.

"Yes, I do indeed! It was quite an experience for me yesterday," she replied. "I was very impressed with the informality of the occasion. Everybody was welcomed, but no one expected to be looked after – and what a lot of friends you invited! Was the Puja being celebrated in other families as well?"

Mrs Datta explained: "Satyanarayan Puja is rather special in the sense that, unlike other pujas, it does not have to be celebrated on a specific day. It is held in honour of Lord Vishnu and can take place on any day that is convenient. The family performs the Puja with a particular object: usually for peace of mind, and for the well-being of the family.

"A significant feature of the Puja is the sharing of the mixture of flour, sugar, ghee and banana which is offered to the god. We call it 'sirni'. During the worship hymns are sung in praise of Vishnu describing his heroic deeds and his greatness. It is very much a family occasion and not a big festival. Vishnu being the Lord Protector, his blessings are invoked for peace and safety and to deliver the family from danger and disaster."

"I see! I thought yesterday was Satyanarayan Puja Day," said Anna. "Was there a specific reason for having the Puja?"

Mrs Datta smiled and said, "It is difficult to explain, but I hope you will understand. You see, I feel restless at times with thoughts of home. My father died soon after I came to Britain. It happened so suddenly that I was not able to see him in the last days of his life. It affected me badly as I was very close to him. The excitement of living in Britain was overshadowed by a feeling of loneliness. This feeling, instead of fading, has been growing within me ever since. So I turned to Vishnu for help. I always feel better after offering my prayers to him during a Satyanarayan Puja."

Anna was a bit embarrassed. She thought it had probably been tactless of her to have asked such a question.

She was about to apologize when Mrs Datta said, "I am sorry, Anna, if I have given you the impression that I regret staying in Britain. That is not so, but modern living does make great demands on our day-to-day life and in meeting them we often come under a lot of physical and mental pressure. It would be foolish not to recognize that. After all, there is as much to be learned from the hardships as from the comforts of life."

"I agree," said Anna, relieved that she didn't have to say any more. Sikha, Goutam and Mr Datta had remained silent while Mrs Datta was speaking.

As Anna wanted to change the subject in order to lighten the atmosphere, she said: "Last week Mr Radcliffe, our careers teacher, came to speak to our class. He just wanted to know if we had any thoughts about our future. All five of the Asian boys and girls told him that they wanted to go to university. Sumitra definitely wants to study Law. They seem to take their studies seriously. I admire them for it, and often wonder how they develop this attitude."

"Let me tell you how," said Mr Datta, sitting up. "A long time ago, there was a learned Brahmin named Chanakya who acted as adviser to Emperor Chandragupta. He wrote a manual of advice which, although over two thousand years old, seems most appropriate to our times.

"Chanakya said that there cannot be any comparison between a king and a learned person. The former is respected only in his own kingdom, but the latter is revered everywhere.

"The stars complement the moon, wives their husbands, and the kingdom its monarch, but learning complements all.

"A mother and father are a child's enemies if they have not

145

educated their child, for without education the child stands out in a learned assembly like a crane in the midst of swans.

"Most parents place a high value on life and bring up their children in the tradition of the great Chanakya. His words of wisdom and advice are passed on from one generation to the next. Now that you have heard them, you may also spread them amongst your friends!"

"I certainly will! I would like to hear it all again, please." Anna's enthusiasm delighted everyone, and Mr Datta was only too happy to oblige. Mrs Datta laughed and got up to fetch another round of cold drinks.

As Mr Datta finished speaking, Anna commented, "The wise man's thoughts on education are very sound indeed. Are there any other principles you follow in your daily life?"

Both Goutam and Sikha responded together. "Respect," they said and looked at each other, smiling.

Sikha explained, "When I was learning to read I came across sentences in my readers like 'Always obey your parents', 'Naren is a good boy. He does what his parents ask him to do' and so on. These simple instructions had a deep effect on me because they were printed words, in a book which was blessed by the goddess Saraswati. Then I learned about Iswar Chandra, a vastly learned man who lived in Bengal in the nineteenth century. His knowledge and wisdom earned him the titles of **Vidyasagar**, which means 'ocean of learning', and **Pandit**, which means 'learned' or 'teacher'. Everyone knows the story of how Vidyasagar once swam across the dangerous floods of the River Damodar to his village just because his mother had repeatedly asked him to be home for a family occasion!"

Goutam interrupted her, saying: "I first became aware of respect at the time of Durga Puja. I could see how deeply people felt about the goddess Durga as Mother. Then, after the immersion ceremony on the last day, Vijaya Dashami Day, the same feeling of respect was transferred to our own mothers, fathers and all the elders. The practice of touching the elders' feet or greeting them with folded hands also made me respectful towards others when I was a child."

"But the terms of respect are learned by children as they grow up within the extended family," said Mr Datta.

"Can you tell me a bit more about the extended family please?"

146

asked Anna. "I have often heard about it but haven't really understood its significance."

"It is quite simple, really," replied Mr Datta. "An average British family comprises the father, the mother and their children. They live in a two- or three-bedroomed house or flat. As soon as the children are ready to look after themselves, they leave their parents and set up their own homes. Parents expect their children to leave home once they are self-sufficient. Within these small units the children have contact with only three or four people. Very few have their grandparents living with them.

"With a Hindu family, however, it is a very different story. As I look back to my own childhood days I can vividly recall the early years of my life in our ancestral home. My grandfather died when I was about six but I can still remember him as someone with a dominating personality. After his death my grandmother assumed the position of head of the family. She had the final word in every decision jointly taken within the family.

"While my grandparents were alive there were three generations of people living in the same house. There were also my uncles and aunts and their children. The family and the village elders commanded a lot of respect and the children could learn a great deal just by observing the family traditions. Our ancestral home provided security for all and there was a lot of sharing between the children and the adults. Hardly anyone ever lived alone."

"Weren't there problems with so many people living together?" Anna asked.

Mrs Datta answered this question, saying: "Yes, there were problems. Sometimes a lot of adults would get involved in settling trivial differences between children. There wasn't much privacy, either, and we all need to spend some time alone. The women, particularly the young wives, had to be careful to behave correctly in the presence of their elders. Nevertheless, when I compare those drawbacks with the many trying situations that confront us over here, I yearn for the peace of mind I enjoyed in the security of our home. There are disadvantages in living within a large family, but the advantages far outweigh them if the family happens to be a thoughtful and open-minded one. Both my husband and I were fortunate in this regard. As we grew up, we both learned to respect our elders; to value education; to share, and work out compromises within the family, and to make a conscious effort, along

147

with everyone else, to develop our understanding of our faith, worship and customs.

"Goutam and Sikha are lucky since they, too, derived the benefits of living a traditional family life before coming to Britain. Indian parents enjoy a very privileged position. Those of us with parents living in India visit them fairly regularly. Such visits have kept our families together although we have lived apart for many years. Many Hindus emigrated to Africa thirty or forty years ago, but were compelled to leave their homes in the late sixties and seventies owing to political upheavals in certain African countries.

Above and opposite: Asian families arriving at Gatwick Airport from Kenya, 1968

They left Africa to make Britain their home and many brought their elderly parents to live with them. Over here the houses are small and at times it is inconvenient to have elderly people living in the family, but this is done without much fuss because of the love, respect and gratitude we have for our parents."

"I think I now have a much clearer picture of the extended family system," said Anna. "It's difficult for me to imagine what it would be like to live with so many people. It would take a while to get used to."

Goutam said, "It's great, Anna, especially, as Mummy said, if it is a nice, well-adjusted family. For me it was wonderful to live among so many people. A child's mind is influenced by the example set by the elders. Besides, our family extended beyond our immediate family and included virtually the whole village."

"How do you mean?" asked Anna, curious.

"You see, in our custom, we do not call our elders by their first names," explained Goutam. "It is considered disrespectful to do so. We always call them 'Brother', 'Sister', 'Uncle', 'Aunt' or 'Gran', for example. Thus, someone who wasn't familiar with this custom would think all the people in the village were related to each other! Not only that, we also add 'Babu' (equivalent of 'Mr') or 'Devi' (goddess) after their name when we address a man or a

149

woman whom we don't know all that well. The pronouns in the second and third persons – you, he/she, they – and their adjectives – your, his/her, their – all vary according to a person's status."

"It sounds very complicated, but I could probably follow if you gave me an example."

"An example!" Sikha exclaimed. "But you don't understand Bengali!"

"I know, but I'm sure it would be possible to recognize the difference just by listening. Besides, I think I have picked up enough Bengali to be able to start learning seriously," Anna persisted. There was a note of challenge in her voice.

Mrs Datta came to her rescue. "Of course it is possible, Anna. Let me give you some examples. Can you repeat what you said to your friend Sumitra when you met her for the very first time?"

"Oh, no! Not that again!" It embarrassed Anna to recall the incident.

"Never mind what happened," smiled Mrs Datta. "Just tell me what you said."

"I said, 'Sumitra, tumi kamon achho?'"

"Perfect! That's the right thing to say if you are addressing a friend," said Mrs Datta, "but as an elder (being your friend's mother) I would probably have been offended by that form of address. Had I been in Sumitra's place you would have changed 'tumi' to 'apni' and 'achho' to 'achhen' and said, 'Apni kamon achhen?' Similarly, to address a very close friend or someone much younger, you could change those words to 'tui' and 'achhis' and say, 'Tui kamon achhis?' but you wouldn't even dream of saying that to me or my husband!"

Mr Datta burst out laughing imagining the situation and said, "That calls for a nice cup of tea! You carry on with your Bengali lesson while I make it."

Mrs Datta continued: "As you can see, Anna, the terms 'apni', 'tumi', and 'tui' are used to indicate a very formal relationship, a less formal one and a very familiar relationship between two or more persons talking to each other. The verbs also change accordingly."

"It is definitely far more complicated than using 'you' as we do in English," Anna remarked.

"Yes, I agree with you there," replied Mrs Datta. "We also have more vowels and consonants in our alphabet, with signs to

150

indicate different sounds, and a much larger vocabulary. In Bengali, there is certainly a lot more to learn at first, but once mastered the language is much more flexible and conveys ideas far more precisely than English."

Mr Datta returned with the tea and cakes and sat down. "Well, what do you think of our language, Anna?" he asked.

"I like it very much. I've decided to learn it seriously. It will be a bit of a struggle to start with, but I shall persevere."

"I can assure you that you will not regret it," Mr Datta encouraged her. "We have a rich cultural heritage. Literature, music, dance and painting dominate our lives. The festivals you have attended have already shown you that, but in order to appreciate the many aspects of our culture and our home life you ought to know the language."

"I have been visiting you for just over a year now," said Anna. "I have become familiar with some of your customs and your way of thinking. You have settled in Britain, perhaps permanently, but I often wonder how you fill the gap between the life you left behind in India and your present one. The festivals I've been to made me feel as though I were in a different land. But then, I was experiencing them for the first time. Do you feel like that too? Are occasional festivals enough? If not, what else do you do?"

"You have an enquiring mind, Anna," Mrs Datta said gently. "You are a sensitive and observant girl with a mature outlook. We must do our best to answer all your questions. I shall tell you my own views and the others may interrupt if they wish.

"First, I must say that we have been lucky that both Goutam and Sikha were old enough to understand our culture and tradition when they left India. They knew their mother tongue well. They have also had the benefit of living in a stable family group. Those religious festivals which you have attended help them to recall some of their past experiences.

"Secondly, we cannot expect to develop every aspect of our life-style in keeping with our traditions while living in Britain. There are too many obstacles. Hence we are always having to make adjustments between two cultures – the one we came from and the one in which we now live. It is relatively easy for people who have a good understanding of one of these cultures to adjust to the other, but those who have little knowledge of either find it extremely difficult to do so.

151

"Mahatma Gandhi said, 'I do not want my house to be surrounded by walls and my windows blocked up. I want the cultures of all lands to be blown about my house as freely as possible. But I refuse to be blown off my feet by any.' He could say this because he had a strong belief in his own tradition and values, but unfortunately many people do get blown off their feet. They are not sure what they should or should not observe, uphold, practise and accept while living alongside another culture and a different way of life. One must know how to make a sensible compromise."

Mr Datta said, "I agree with you. I have lived in Britain for more than twenty years and have seen many changes in society. When I first came here I had the excitement of experiencing new things in a new country. I went out of my way to introduce myself to British people. They were eager to learn about India and the Hindu way of life."

"I am surprised that people were interested in learning about Hindu culture at that time," Sikha remarked.

"Well, a lot of them were, but there were also those who did not care," replied Mr Datta. "You see, the war had ended only fifteen years earlier and India had achieved independence. The officers in the British armed forces, the Civil Service, etc. were returning home after spending a few years in India. Their stories circulated through their own families, friends and colleagues. Many of these stories were fabricated and gave a distorted picture of Indian social and religious customs, although many were accurate. After all, not everyone who went to India went there to study Hinduism or the Indian culture. But surprisingly enough, some of them did just that! They were learned people who returned to Britain after acquiring a vast amount of knowledge of the country, its history and culture, and wrote many books. The contribution of such people was immense and provided the basis on which the friendship and understanding between India and Britain was to grow. I have nothing but the highest regard for them.

"As for the majority, well, they went there as soldiers, administrators, missionaries and traders. While going about their business they experienced both the good and the bad in Indian life and their stories only reflected their personal views.

"In the early days, while visiting my friends at Christmas or over a Sunday lunch, I used to be asked questions, some of a personal

152

nature, that embarrassed me no end. But such questions, as I quickly realized, were put quite innocently, simply to confirm whether or not their information was correct."

"It must have been a very uncomfortable situation for you," Anna sympathized.

"It wasn't as awful as you think," replied Mr Datta. "I had to be patient. I tried to understand their point of view. I had to explain why I agreed or disagreed with their remarks, but I was careful not to enter into any unnecessary arguments. I also had to learn to ignore a lot of things which were said out of sheer ignorance. I soon realized how fortunate I was in my education and upbringing in India, and I was thankful for my faith in my religion and way of life. I was able to make many friends in this way. They were educated people who recognized the fact that I spoke from a position of strength and had a lot to offer to the growth of our mutual understanding."

Anna said, "I'm still not sure what you did before your family arrived – and what you do now – to keep in touch with your own cultural traditions, apart from celebrating festivals, of course."

Mr Datta replied, "Both my wife and I were trying to explain to you that in our situation it is important to be well-versed in our own customs and practices. That has helped us cope with the demands of the Western way of life, and our children have been lucky in this regard, too. But as regards keeping in touch, well, we have to go out and seize every opportunity that might help us.

"A lot of things have happened in Britain since the early sixties and the changes that have taken place in the last ten years would have been unthinkable when I arrived here. We now visit the Commonwealth Institute in Kensington High Street regularly. I have been going there since it opened in 1962. Apart from the permanent exhibition galleries, the Institute holds talks, seminars, films and cultural events. The recent presentation of the Spring Festivals of India compèred by Rani Singh, the well-known story-teller, was a striking example of the progress in cultural activities achieved by schoolchildren in Britain. The music, singing and dance were of a very high standard. The performance was given by children from Indian community schools which have started up all over the country in recent years.

"I would say that the Festival of India held in 1982 made a great impact on the cultural life of Britain. Practically all aspects of our

HFB-K

Dancers from the school founded by Rabindra Nath Tagore in Santiniketan, West Bengal, perform at a primary school in Devon.

way of life were on view to thousands of people from Britain and abroad during the festival. Our former prime minister, the late Mrs Indira Gandhi, said, 'The Festival of India which has succeeded beyond our wildest hopes has not been just a show-window for India but has actively created interest in India.'"

Mrs Datta added, "We have already talked about the importance of learning our own language. There are many encouraging signs in this respect as well. At the community schools regular classes are held in Gujarati, Bengali, Urdu, Hindi and so on."

"Really?" cried Anna. "Do you think I could attend one? Would they accept me?"

"Of course they would," Mrs Datta assured her. "In fact, they would be delighted. You could come with us to the community school we are closely involved with. Classes are held every Sunday. In fact, all community schools are open during weekends and on some evenings. Parents and children attend whenever it is most convenient for them."

Goutam said, "You may have noticed that we hardly ever speak English within the family. We have made a pact to speak only Bengali, unless it is absolutely necessary to use English."

Sikha confirmed her brother's remarks, saying, "And it is working quite well. It is only Daddy and I who slip up at times! But I do enjoy going to the Bengali school. Goutam and Mummy teach there but I just help the younger children with their reading and handwriting."

Mrs Datta said, "The importance of learning one's mother tongue is being realized now, both at school and by parents. The ability to communicate in one's mother tongue and in English is a great asset and children do not acquire such skills by themselves just because they have a different language at home. Parents have to give their children a lot of support by talking to them, helping them to explain things properly, telling them stories at bedtime and, if possible, providing means for the appreciation of music. When parents cannot afford the time beause of other family or business commitments it is the community schools that give the children the opportunity to learn their own language.

"We learned English before we came to Britain but we were able to adjust to the way of life only because we had faith in our own ability to do so. Our language and our own culture gave us that confidence."

Goutam recalled his experience on his very first morning in Britain: "It was early Sunday morning. I had no idea how long I had slept after that long flight from Calcutta, but I sat bolt upright in bed when I heard a Hindi song playing right by my pillow! It was a song from a film, one I knew very well, but I hadn't expected to hear it after flying thousands of kilometres to England! It was Daddy's idea of a joke, you see. He put his transistor radio by my pillow so that I could hear the Radio Four programme for Asian listeners called *Make Yourself At Home*, presented by Ashok Rampal. Daddy laughed at my reaction, then sat on my bed, and we had a long chat. He was obviously very happy that we were all together at last.

"Next we watched the BBC 1 presentation of *Nai Zindagi Naya Jivan*, which is now called *Asian Magazine*. What a surprise it was for us on our first day in Britain! And now, looking back, I can see how reassuring it was, too. We had just arrived at our new home, but the transition from India could not have been smoother. On our first morning we had listened to our own songs, watched our own programme on television, eaten our own food at lunch and chatted non-stop in our own language. It was only in the afternoon, when Daddy suggested that we ought to go out for a walk, that we felt for the first time that we were in England.

"It was the month of August and the four weeks following our arrival were packed with excitement. We visited no end of places in and around London. A visit to Lord's fulfilled one of my childhood dreams. By the time the schools reopened in September, and Sikha and I arrived at our respective schools for enrolment, we stood there like two seasoned veterans. It was, however, only at school that our real life in Britain began. It started as we made contact with our classmates, our teachers and the other members of staff. Some friendships formed naturally, while others began with bitterness and misunderstanding. We learned to fight our own battles. The system of education was quite different to the one we had known in India, of course."

Goutam paused for a moment, then went on: "As a family we have been extremely fortunate in settling down so easily, but there are people – at my school, for example – for whom it has not been easy at all."

"But what an exciting life you've had!" exclaimed Anna.

"Yes, it has been quite exciting for me, too," said Mrs Datta. "When I was getting ready to come to Britain I was very nervous about beginning a new life in a foreign country. We prepared ourselves as thoroughly as possible to integrate into British society. Surprisingly enough, that part has been relatively easy. We are now having to make quite an effort to retain and develop the values of our own culture and traditions."

Mr Datta nodded in agreement and said, "I feel that although the well-known proverb 'When in Rome do as Rome does' helps us develop the right attitude towards our host country and its culture, everything should be done in moderation and with a clear conscience. In this way there will be respect on both sides."

It was nearly half past eight. The large red disc of the setting sun was disappearing behind the trees, but it was still light. It had been a long and pleasant afternoon in the garden. Anna stood up to say goodbye and reluctantly left for home.

QUESTIONS AND PROJECTS

Chapters 17–19

1   Holi is one of the most popular Hindu festivals. Find out more about it and paint scenes to illustrate your account.

2   At Holi caste and social barriers are forgotten. At the Roman festival of Saturnalia, on the other hand, social positions were completely reversed. Write a short description of this ancient festival.

3   New Year is celebrated at different times by different faiths. Draw up a calendar for the coming year to show the dates of the Christian, Hindu, Jewish, Muslim and Sikh New Year.

4   Arrange a class discussion about the upbringing of children in a traditional Hindu family, with particular attention to their attitudes to education, their elders and their religion. Make comparisons with the traditions of other cultures.

5   Does the idea of living in an extended family appeal to you? Give your reasons.

6   Consider the quotation from Mahatma Gandhi on p.152. What do you think he meant?

7   You have been introduced to someone who has just arrived in Britain and is getting used to living here. Suggest ways of helping them to adjust to their new home without giving up their own customs.

8   Goutam said, "It was, however, only at school that our real life in Britain began. ... We learned to fight our own battles." Interview friends from different faiths or cultures and record their experiences.

Resources/Useful Addresses

Bharatiya Vidya Bhavan
(Institute of Indian Culture)
4a Castletown Road
London W14 9HQ

The Hindu Centre
39 Grafton Terrace
London NW5 4JA

The Commonwealth Institute
Kensington High Street
London W8 6NQ

Hindu Cultural Society
321 Leeds Road
Bradford

Ramakrishna Vedanta Centre
Unity House, Blind Lane
Bourne End
Bucks SL8 5LG

When writing to any of the above addresses for information, please remember to enclose a stamped, addressed envelope for the reply.

BOOKS FOR PUPILS
Divali, Howard Marsh. Living Festivals series, R.M.E.P.
Faiths and Festivals, Martin Palmer. Ward Lock.
The Hindu World, Patricia Bahree. Macdonald.
Hindu Gods and Goddesses, A. G. Mitchell. H.M.S.O.
Hindus and Hinduism, Partha and Swasti Mitter. Wayland.
Holi, Janis Hannaford. Living Festivals series, R.M.E.P.
Man of Peace:Mahatma Gandhi, Audrey Constant. R.M.E.P.
Milestones:Rites of Passage in a Multi-faith Community, Celia Collinson and Campbell Miller. Edward Arnold.

Myths and Legends of India, Veronica Ions. Hamlyn.
Ramayana, William Buck. Mentor.
Saraswati Puja, Sauresh Ray. Living Festivals series, R.M.E.P.
The Way of the Hindu, S. Yogashananda. Hulton.

BOOKS FOR TEACHERS
Festivals and Holidays of India, P. Thomas. Taraporevela.
Hinduism, K. M. Sen. Pelican.
A History of India, Vol. 1, Romila Thapar. Pelican.
A History of India, Vol. 2, Percival Spear. Pelican.
Indian Mythology, Veronica Ions. Newnes.
The Life of Mahatma Gandhi, Louis Fischer. Granada.
Ramayana and Mahabharata. Dent.
Religion in the Multi-Faith School, W. Owen Cole. Hulton.

SLIDES
Hindu Mythology, Temples and Religious Ceremonies, and others, available from Ann and Bury Peerless, 22 King's Avenue, Minnis Bay, Birchington-on-Sea, Kent CT7 9QL.
Hindu Worship; A Hindu Wedding; The Hindu Temple and Its Symbols and others, available from The Slide Centre, Ilton, Ilminster, Somerset TA19 9HS.

VIDEO AND FILMS
All the following can be obtained from P.E.P. (Pergamon Educational Productions) through R.M.E.P.:
Exploring Religious Ideas in a Primary School: Through a Hindu Festival (Saraswati Puja). ILEA.
Hinduism through the eyes of Hindu children. CEM Video.
I'm Here (Bengali boys discuss what it means to be part of a minority group). ILEA.

POSTERS
Hindu Festivals; Birth Rites; Marriage Rites; Holy Places and others. Pictorial Charts Education Trust, 27 Kirchen Road, London W13 0UD.

RELIGIOUS ARTEFACTS
Articles of Faith, 123 Neville Road, Salford M7 0PP.

Glossary

Agni the god of fire; sacred fire lit in temples, etc.

alpana patterns drawn on the floor with fingers dipped in a thick paste of powdered rice and water.

Anna Prashan ceremony of a child's first feeding with solid food.

arati special form of prayer offered to a deity in which a five-branched lamp is used.

Aryans early Indo-European settlers.

asan mat used for sitting on.

asanas Yoga positions.

asoucha state of impurity that affects the relatives in particular following a death or birth within the family.

Atharva Veda last of the four Vedas, containing a collection of magical formulae.

Atman self or soul.

Aurobindo, Sri (1872–1950) Indian philosopher and spiritual leader.

baran Bengali ritual observed especially to offer greetings of welcome.

Besant, Dr Annie (1847–1933) British religious thinker who helped in the Indian Freedom Movement and became president of the Indian National Congress.

betel-nut supari or areca nut. Used for chewing, sliced and wrapped in a betel leaf

160

	smeared with lime, often flavoured with cloves, etc.
Bhagwat Gita	literally, "Songs of the Lord/Creator". Taken from the Mahabharata. Popularly known simply as the Gita.
bou-bhaat	(Bengali) feast held in honour of a bride.
Brahma	the Creator. God associated with Vishnu and Shiva.
Brahman	Truth; all-pervading God.
Brahmana	prose section in each of the four Vedas, dealing with sacrifices and rites.
Brahmin	member of the priestly caste.
Bose, Subhas	(1897–1945) Indian national leader and founder of the Indian National Army. Known as 'Netaji' (Leader of the Nation).
chapati	pancake-shaped wheaten bread.
Charanamrita	holy water used to wash a deity's feet and sipped by the devotees as nectar.
choli	woman's blouse or bodice, worn under a sari.
Choti	or (Bengali) **Tikee**. Tuft of hair worn at the back of the head by some Hindu males.
dal	pulses.
dhoti	length of material worn by men as lower garment.
diva	or **deep**. Small oil-burning lamp, usually made of clay.
Divali	Festival of Lights.
Dravidians	race believed by many to be the primitive inhabitants of India who eventually settled in the Deccan.
dupatta	length of lightweight material passed over a woman's shoulder to cover the upper part of her body; also acts as a head-scarf.
Durga	the goddess also known as Parvati, wife of Shiva. Appears in warrior form destroying the demon Mahishasura.

161

Durga Puja	*see* Dussera.
Dussera	Durga Puja or Navaratri (Nine Nights). Festival held in honour of Durga.
Ganapati	or **Ganapathy**. Literally, "Leader of the Multitude". Name given to Ganesha.
Gandhi, M. K.	(1869–1948) also called "the Mahatma" and "Father of the Nation". Indian national leader and social reformer, largely responsible for India's independence. Fought apartheid in South Africa and untouchability in India and preached ahimsa (non-violence).
Gandhi, Mrs Indira	(1917–1984) former prime minister of India; daughter of Pandit Nehru.
Ganesh Chaturthi	Lord Ganesha's birthday.
Ganesha	elephant-headed son of Shiva. The god of wisdom and success.
gangasthi	throwing the bones into the River Ganges after cremation.
gayey holood	(Bengali) ritual of smearing the bride and groom with turmeric paste before the wedding ceremony.
ghanta	bell.
ghatak	(Bengali) professional matchmaker.
ghee	clarified butter.
godhuli lagna	the auspicious period of "cattle-dust" – dusk.
gramadevata	village deity.
guru	teacher, mentor.
Harijans	literally, "children of God". Name given to the Untouchables by Gandhi.
Hate Khadi	(Bengali) ceremony at which a child is formally initiated into learning.
Holi	Festival of Colour.
homa	ceremony in which ghee is burnt.
Indra	leader of the gods.
ishtadevata	personal deity; image carried in a wallet, set in a ring, etc.
Jagannath	guardian deity of Orissa. Lord of the Universe, a form of Vishnu.

162

Kailasa	divine home of Shiva.
kajal	(Bengali) black eye make-up made by collecting soot on an oily surface above the flame of a lamp.
Kali	warlike wife of Shiva.
Kali Puja	festival held in honour of the goddess Kali.
Karma	deeds which determine one's status in the next incarnation.
kol-bor	*see* nit-bor.
Krishna	an incarnation of Vishnu.
Kshatriya	member of the warrior caste.
kuladevata	guardian deity worshipped within the family.
kumkum	cosmetic with which women paint a red dot between the eyebrows.
kurta	man's tunic.
ladoo	round sweets.
Lakshmi	the goddess of wealth and prosperity.
Lakshmi-Narayan	Vishnu as Lakshmi's husband.
Lakshmi Purana	legends about Lakshmi narrated in verse form.
madhuparka	part of the marriage ceremony in which honey (madhu) is offered to the bridegroom.
Mahabharata	one of the two great epic poems of Hinduism (the other is the Ramayana). Tells the story of two branches of the same family who quarrel over their right to the throne.
Mahadeva	Shiva.
Mahastami	eighth day of Dussera.
Mahatma	literally, "great soul". *See* Gandhi.
Makar Sankranti	festival held in the ninth month (Pausha), when the sun enters the sign of Capricorn.
Manasha	the serpent goddess.
mantra	holy syllables uttered while performing a puja.
moksha	release of the soul from all earthly ties.

163

moodi or **mudi**	(Bengali). Rice heated over sand to make rice crispies.
mukhagni	cremation rite in which a torch is touched to the head of the deceased.
Naba Barsha	Bengali New Year.
Naga Panchami	day on which serpent worship takes place.
Naidu, Mrs Sarojini	(1879–1949) well-known Indian poet and political thinker.
Naivedya	offerings to a deity.
Namaskaar	popular form of greeting, spoken with palms together in an attitude of respect.
Nandi	Lord Shiva's mount, a bull.
Nataraja	the Lord of Dance, Lord Shiva.
Navaratri	*see* Dussera.
Nehru, Pandit Jawaharlal	(1889–1964) first prime minister of India and father of Indira Gandhi.
nit-bor or **kol-bor**	(Bengali). Small boy acting as the bridegroom's companion.
pan	leaf of the betel.
Pandit	learned man.
Pandit, Mrs V.	(1900–) Indian ambassador to the U.S.S.R. and to the U.S.A. and high commissioner in London. Sister of Jawaharlal Nehru.
phoolsajya	literally, "bed of flowers". First night a couple spend together after their wedding.
pidi	(Bengali) slightly raised wooden plank used as a seat.
pindadaan	rite of offering rice-balls to the spirit of a dead person.
pradip	(Bengali) oil-lamp, usually made of clay, but sometimes brass.
prasaad	food offered to a deity and later shared among the worshippers.
preeti bhojan	(Bengali) feast, usually for a wedding.
puja	worship.
Puranas	legends of the gods and goddesses.
Purnima	day of the full moon.

Pushpanjali	floral offerings to a deity.
Radha	consort of Krishna.
Radhakrishnan, Dr S.	(1888–1975) eminent scholar, philosopher and former president of India.
Rakhi	amulet made of silk, cork, mica and tinsel tied on the wrist.
Rakhi Purnima	festival held on the full-moon day of the fourth month (Shravana), during which Rakhis are tied on people's wrists.
Rama Krishna, Sri	(1836–1886). Hindu religious leader. He taught that all religions are, in essence, the same and that all are true. Swami Vivekananda was his most famous disciple.
Ramayana	one of the two great epic poems of Hinduism (the other is the Mahabharata). It describes the banishment of Rama (an incarnation of Vishnu) and the capture of his wife Sita by Ravana, and tells how Rama defeated the demon Ravana, rescued Sita and regained his throne.
Rath Yatra	Car Festival of Lord Jagannath.
Rig Veda	first of the four Vedas, containing a collection of hymns in praise of the gods.
rishis	sages.
Roy, Raja Ram Mohan	(1772–1833) eminent scholar and religious and social reformer. Founder of the Brahmo-Samaj (Society of believers in the one Self-existent Deity). Promoted Western education, especially science and mathematics, in India.
sadhu	holy man.
Sama Veda	second of the four Vedas, containing melodies connected with the hymns in the Rig Veda.
Samhitas	literally, 'collection'. Hymns contained in all four Vedas.
Sanskrit	sacred language of the Hindus.
saptapadi	Seven symbolic steps taken by the bride

	and bridegroom during the wedding ceremony.
Saraswati	goddess of learning and the arts.
Saraswati Puja	festival held to worship the goddess Saraswati.
Satyanarayan Puja	worship within the family of Narayan (Vishnu) as Protector.
shamiana	large canopy, often decorated with brightly coloured patchwork.
shanai	wind instrument similar to a clarinet.
Shastra	holy scriptures.
shila	stone slab.
Shiva	Lord Shiva, the Destroyer. Associated with Brahma (the creator) and Vishnu (the Preserver).
shraddha or shraads	Ceremony in honour of the soul of a dead person in which Brahmins are fed, rites are performed and a feast held, usually between ten and thirty-one days after the cremation.
shubha-dristi	auspicious "exchange of eyes", when the bride removes her veil and looks at the groom (Bengali custom).
shubha-yatra	auspicious journey.
Shudra	member of the lowest caste.
Sindhu	River Indus.
Smriti	literally, "recollection". The Vedic codes relating to law and social conduct.
Sruti	literally, "heard" or "learning by hearing". The Vedas, said to be the word of God as told to the sages.
Swami	holy man. Title of respect.
swastika	holy symbol. Clockwise, 卐 it means "all is well" and represents knowledge and being. Anti-clockwise, 卍 it is the symbol of Kali the destroyer.
Tagore, Rabindra Nath	(1861–1941) great Indian poet, awarded the Nobel prize for literature in 1913.
Tikee	see Choti.
Tilak	holy mark on forehead.

166

topor	(Bengali) bridegroom's hat, made of pith.
uloodhyani	(Bengali) sound produced by quivering the tongue around the lips made to announce a happy event.
Untouchables	outcastes.
Upanayana	ceremony in which a boy of high caste is given the sacred thread.
Upanishads	sacred verses at the end of the Vedas.
Upavita	sacred thread.
Vaishnavs	devotees of Vishnu.
Vaishya	member of the merchant caste.
Varna Shrestha	the superior caste, the Brahmins.
Vasant Panchami	the fifth day of spring.
Vedas	the Samhitas: the Rig Veda, Sama Veda, Yajur Veda and Atharva Veda; the four main sections of the oldest Hindu scriptures.
Vidyasagar	(1820–1891) literally, "Ocean of Knowledge". Title given to Iswar Chandra, educationist and social reformer of Bengal.
Vijaya Dashami	tenth and last day of Dussera.
Vishnu	the Preserver. God associated with Brahma and Shiva.
Viswakarma	the architect god.
Vivekananda, Swami	(1862–1902) first Hindu missionary to visit the West. Born Narendra Nath Datta.
Vratas	fasts and rituals held to worship deities, usually with a specific object, e.g. for prosperity, to cure a disease.
yajna	sacrifices.
Yajur Veda	third of the four Vedas, containing a collection of formulae for performing sacrifices.
Yoga	literally, "union"; the control of body and mind. This may be achieved through Bhakti (devotion), Jnana (knowledge) or Karma (action) Yoga.

167